TREASURE ISLAND

Almost a pantomime

GW00702681

Stewart Auty

ACTI SCI p1.
ACTI SC2 p31

ACT2 SC2 p71
ACT2 SC3 p79

Published by Playstage
United Kingdom.

An imprint of Write Publications Ltd

www.playsforadults.com

© 2010 Playstage
An imprint of Write Publications Ltd.

All rights pertaining to this play or any part of this play are the property of the author
and managed by Playstage, PO Box 52, AXMINSTER, EX13 5WB, United Kingdom.
Licences to perform this play are issued by Playstage upon payment of a fee. To give a
reading or performance of this play without possession of a licence issued by Playstage
is an infringement of copyright.

PLEASE CHECK THAT THIS PLAY IS AVAILABLE FOR PERFORMANCE BEFORE
COMMENCING REHEARSALS.

This play is protected under the Copyright Laws currently existing in every country
throughout the world. All rights pertaining to stage; motion picture; radio; audio; digi-
tal; television; public reading and translation into foreign languages are the property of
the author and his or her agents. No part of this play may be copied or stored in any
format without permission from the copyright holders. No part of this play may be al-
tered in any way without permission from the copyright holders.

Designed by Kate Lowe, Greensands Graphics
Printed by Creeds Ltd, Bridport, Dorset

Note to producers about staging "Treasure Island"

The essential story of Treasure Island is there (somewhere) but elements have been added in to make it more like a pantomime or 'spoof'. Therefore, the cast have to play it with a certain amount of gusto; plenty of audience awareness and interaction; and a lot of tongue firmly in cheek.

THE ACTORS

In keeping with the needs of most drama groups, we have made most of the pirates female. Any non-speaking chorus (required throughout the action) should be female as well, of any age. Bring out your nasty side, ladies!

DOUBLING OF PARTS

With the male actors, there is scope for the doubling of parts. Our suggestion, based upon the amount of time that the first character would have to change into the second character, would be as follows:

BILLY BONES/BEN GUNN

BLACK DOG/LONG JOHN SILVER

BLIND PEW/CAPTAIN SMOLLETT

The SQUIRE and the DOCTOR would not be able to double as any other characters. Doubling in this way would reduce the need for men to five.

COSTUMES

Dirty, scruffy pirates with, perhaps the odd nod to their gender (leopard print leggings rather than pantaloons, perhaps? Curlers in their hair, in front of their bandana? The possibilities are endless.)

CAPTAIN SMOLLETT, SQUIRE PEGG and DOCTOR LIVESEY should be smart, eighteenth century costume with powdered wigs. SMOLLETT should be dressed as a sea captain, of course.

JIM LARD should be dressed in clean knee breeches, shirt and waistcoat with his/her hair tied back in a pony tail.

BLIND PEW should wear a black cloak and large black hat, dark glasses and carry a white stick.

BEN GUNN is dressed, mostly, in animal skins.

Mrs HAWKINS and RUBY should be dressed in long dresses – as the only females who are not actual pirates. Similarly, Ms JOBSWORTH should be dressed in a long skirt and top with a fluorescent safety waistcoat on and carrying or wearing a hard hat.

SCENERY

(See SET PLANS) The idea is to have a set that looks as though it is made of wood, so that various parts of it can be taken away to make the ship and the island. The whole of ACT 1 takes place in the Admiral Benbow Inn. Set changes can then take place in the interval.

MUSIC

Suggested songs in the text are as follows:

The Admiral Benbow; A Rovin'; Lily The Pink *(The Scaffold)*; What shall we do with a Drunken Sailor?; I'll(We'll) be Watching You *(The Police)*; Wild Rover; Money, Money, Money *(ABBA)*; Blow The Man Down; The Female of The Species Is Deadlier Than the Male *(The Walker Brothers)*; Sailing *(Rod Stewart)*; Sisters Are Doing It For Themselves *(Annie Lennox)* ; Row, Row, Row, Your Boat; Girls Just Wanna Have Fun *(Cyndi Lauper)*; She *(Cheese) (Charles Aznavour)*; Blue (Gold) Is The Colour *(Chelsea F.C.)*; I Just Can't Get You Out Of My Head *(Kylie)*.

Backing tracks for all of these songs can be found on the internet for a modest fee. Try a company like www.ameritz.co.uk Sheet music can be found at any good sheet music supplier. Drama groups performing this play can feel free to eliminate/ change or add to the songs.

SOUND EFFECTS

Gunshots are needed in Acts 1 and 11. These can be done manually, with starting pistols (more than one will be needed) or purchased from the internet as mp3 downloads. Try www.sound-effects-library.com

TREASURE ISLAND

CAST *(In order of appearance)*

BILLY BONES*	Drunken old pirate aged 60+
MRS HAWKINS	Landlady of the Admiral Benbow Inn aged 50+
JIM LARD	Mrs Hawkins' son aged about 15 *Immie (Imogen)*
RUBY O'RILEY	Serving wench, any age. *Annie (Anastasia).*
PRETTY PEARL PLANK	Female pirate, any age.
CUTTHROAT KATY	Female Pirate, any age.
HANDBAG JONES	Female Pirate, any age.
Ms JOBSWORTH	Irritating Health and Safety Inspector, any age.
DOCTOR LIVESEY	Local quack, any age.
BLACK DOG*	Vicious pirate, male, any age.
BLIND PEW*	Blind pirate, elderly.
SQUIRE PEGG*	Local Squire, aged 50+
CAPTAIN SMOLLETT*	Captain of the ship, aged 50+ *Vincent*
LONG JOHN SILVER*	One legged, one eyed, one handed leader of the pirates, aged 50+
BEN GUNN*	Deranged marooned pirate, aged 60+
PIRATES	Assorted non-speaking but singing pirates needed. Any age, any gender.

Denotes parts than can be doubled. (See Production Notes.)

7 female parts (if a woman plays JIM LARD), and maximum 5 male parts if doubling (See Production Notes)

Unlimited numbers of pirate chorus of any age or gender.

TREASURE ISLAND
ACT 1
SCENE 1

The interior of the Admiral Benbow Inn. The set is, basically, wood panelling. (SEE SET PLAN 1) There is an inn sign hanging front stage left which says "Admiral Benbow Inn". Before the lights come up, the inn's customers are drinking heavily, in noisy conversation. There are two or three small tables dotted around the stage with stools/upturned barrels around them. Billy BONES is seated alone at one of the tables, which is centre stage. The tavern bar is stage right and Mrs HAWKINS (MRS H), RUBY and JIM LARD are filling tankards and waiting on tables from this location. There is a ship's bell hanging on a stand on the bar or behind the bar. There is also a drum under the bar, which RUBY uses in the DOCTOR LIVESEY scene. There is a door upstage right which leads to the rest of the establishment and a door upstage left which leads to the street. There are no windows visible on the set. The lights come up and the assembled cast (mostly female pirates) burst into song.

Song 1.

ALL   **The Admiral Benbow**

SEMPR   Come all you seamen bold

               and draw near, and draw near,

               Come all you seamen bold and draw near.

               It is of an admiral's fame,

               O brave Benbow was his name,

               How he fought all on the main,

               you shall hear, you shall hear.

MRS H	*(to audience)* I've interrupted the singing to explain something to you good people gathered here. The more observant of you – and I accept that doesn't include everyone, but the more perceptive of you will have noticed that we've been singing about 'seamen bold'. And some of you might have noticed that strictly speaking, this isn't exactly accurate. Yes, we have some sea men, but there is a considerable female presence in this establishment. The Admiral Benbow Inn is sort of a women's refuge for displaced 'lady' pirates. Women who take to piracy as a career option are not well liked. They're not well liked because basically they're thieves, just like them men pirates. But the dislike goes further than that! It's bordering on hatred, because we women are better at it than the men! Ain't that right, ladies?
PEARL	You bet it is Mrs Hawkins, and it's right generous of you to provide a safe haven for us all, as we've nowhere else to go. We're all sisters together, united by adversity, but all the stronger for it.
MRS H	Now we'll explain more in due course. But I felt I should explain in case any of you lot were having a gender differentiation crisis. Not all is what it seems. So let's carry on, now that little misunderstanding has been clarified. This is verse two!
ALL	*(continuing the song)* Brave Benbow he set sail for to fight, for to fight Brave Benbow he set sail for to fight. Brave Benbow he set sail with a fine and pleasant gale

Get up
& move
DS C

but his captains they turn'd tail

in a fright, in a fright.

The Ruby and Benbow

fought the French, fought the French

The Ruby and Benbow fought the French.

They fought them up and down,

till the blood came trickling down,

Till the blood came trickling down

where they lay, where they lay.

Brave Benbow lost his legs

by chain shot, by chain shot

Brave Benbow lost his legs by chain shot.

Brave Benbow lost his legs,

And all on his stumps he begs,

Fight on my English lads,

'Tis our lot, 'tis our lot.

JIM LARD	*(to audience)* I see lots of you were singing along with us. That's great, we don't mind a bit. In fact it helps, so join in with any of the songs. I'm sure you will know the words! Now let's get on with the story!
MRS H	Let me first introduce you to some of my regular customers. There's Cutthroat Katy – say Hello Katy, and tell the people what you do when you're not into piracy.
KATY	Why, I'm a ship's barber, and I love to cut hair and give the men a shave. I'm always careful when I'm shaving from 'ere to 'ere!

MRS H	But she does make the occasional mistake, hence her nickname of Cutthroat. Next to her is Plank, Pretty Pearl Plank.
PEARL	*(curtsies)* Pleased to make your acquaintance, I'm sure.
MRS H	She has a lovely voice, does Pearl. But I expect you've all heard ... Pearl's a singer.
	And this is "Handbag" Jones.
HANDBAG	So called on account of I always carries a handbag...
KATY	Which always has a brick in it...
PEARL	And she uses it to "handbag" her victims!
RUBY	And my name's Ruby. Ruby O'Riley.
MRS H	Oh, really?
RUBY	No. O'Riley. I serve behind the bar, and generally help around the Inn. My best mate is little Miss Green over there. She's called Teresa, but everyone knows Teresa Green. Ha ha!
MRS H	And this, of course, is my son, Jim Lard. A fine hard-working boy and a credit to me, although I say it myself.
JIM LARD	Thank you, mother.
MRS H	So, there we are. Our merry little establishment is home to many a lady pirate and the occasional male pirate – like him, over there. *(She points to BONES)* Billy Bones. He looks harmless enough, but when he's had a drink or three, he can be quite a handful.
BONES	Yo, ho, ho and a bottle of rum! Another rum, Mrs. Hawkins, if you please.
MRS H	Another rum? You've had more than enough, Billy Bones!

BONES	It's not for you to decide how much I drink! You're just a serving woman, so serve me!
MRS H	I'm no common wench! I own this establishment, and I say you've had enough!
JIM LARD	It wouldn't be so bad if you paid for your drink.
BONES	Careful boy! I may be old and I may be drunk, but I'll clip your ear if you give me any cheek.
JIM LARD	You'll have to catch me first! *(skips away, laughing)*
BONES	*(roaring)* What's keeping you woman? Where's my rum?
MRS H	I've told you! You've had enough!
JIM LARD	And you haven't paid for your last drinks. So what about some money?
BONES	God's teeth! Can't a man have some rest from all the nagging? I'll pay later you cheeky young pup!
JIM LARD	*(to audience)* He's been saying that for the last three weeks, ever since he came here, dragging behind him his old sea chest. He wanted a place which was quiet, off the beaten track, he said. *(confidentially)* Every day he walks up to the cliff top, or sits in the window for hours just looking out. He's a frightened man, I can tell. And when he's drunk – like he is now, he tells such stories of his life at sea. Between you and me, I think he's on the run from someone. Why else would he hide in an all female refuge? Sometimes, when he's asleep, he calls out, or starts singing to himself. "Fifteen men on a dead man's chest, Yo, ho, ho and a bottle of rum!"
BONES	What you mutt'ring about, young Jim Lard?
JIM LARD	*(pointing to audience)* I'm just talking to my friends, that's all.

BONES	Well come over 'ere and talk to me.
	(JIM LARD approaches BONES, who grabs him by the arm.)
BONES	Gotcha! *(mimics JIM LARD)* You'll have to catch me first! Well, I just did!
JIM LARD	Let me go! Ow! You're hurting me!
BONES	I'm not hurting you, I'm reminding you to show me some respect, that's all.
JIM LARD	You'll get some respect when you stop bullying me and start paying your debts.
	(Enter Ms. JOBSWORTH (JW) from the upstage right door. She is a pompous woman wearing a safety helmet, high visibility jacket and carrying a clipboard.)
JW	Stop it at once! You can't behave like that!
BONES	What the devil? This looks like trouble to me. *ELBOW JIM*
JW	I work in the Human Relations department. You can call it H.R., but being a pirate, you probably say 'aitch arrgh!'
BONES	Human relations? Aitch arrgh? What's anything to do with you?
JW	You were clearly bullying the boy. I saw it for myself. Intimidation of a minor is unacceptable.
BONES	You never told me you worked underground, Jim Lard. *(waits, then says to audience)* She said I was bullying a miner. Oh, please yourselves. Last night's audience was quicker on the uptake.
JW	Don't interrupt. Such behaviour will not be tolerated. Jim Lard – here is the telephone number of Childline. If he gives

you any more trouble, ring them and report him. Otherwise contact their website www.childline.com. *(To BONES)* I'm watching you. Any more such behaviour and you will find yourself sent on a Respect for Young Adults course. *(JW exits through the upstage right door.)*

BONES   Interfering old busy-body! *(To JIM LARD)* Now let's not fall out, Jim Lard. We're mates, aren't we? I'll pay my way. Here, come closer. *(He beckons to JIM LARD and looks around furtively)* Can you keep a secret Jim Lard? *(louder)* I said, can you keep a secret?

JIM LARD   It won't be much of a secret if you don't quieten down!

BONES   *(whispers loudly)* I know of an island where treasure is buried ...

JIM LARD   Treasure?

(Upon hearing this word, every woman pirate in the place sits up and takes notice, then leans towards where BONES is sitting)

BONES   Sssh! Be quiet, lad! Walls have ears!

(He looks around quickly over his right shoulder and everyone in that direction quickly pretends to look away and not listen. Then he does the same over his left shoulder and they all look away/ examine their nails/ pretend they're not listening. As soon as he turns back to JIM LARD, they all lean towards him again.)

I know where there's enough gold and silver to more than pay for my stay here.

JIM LARD   Gold and silver, buried, on an island?

BONES	Aye, Jim Lard. But it be Captain Flint's gold, that's why it's a secret! Flint's dead but there's plenty of his men, still alive, who are looking for the treasure map.
JIM LARD	Captain Flint, did you say? The blood thirstiest pirate that ever lived? The same Captain Flint who is rumoured to have killed many of his own men? The Captain Flint…
KATY	*(Getting annoyed)* Oy! He said Captain Flint, didn't he? Give it a rest!
BONES	*(to JIM LARD)* Keep your voice down! There are some here I don't trust. Not a word to anyone, you hear?
JIM LARD	No sir! My lips are sealed. So why don't you go and find the treasure?
BONES	I'm too old now, and I'm not well. My days at sea are over, more's the pity.
Song 2.	**A - Rovin'** *(verses can be edited)*
	(As this is a narrative song, it can be acted out by BONES and RUBY.)
BONES	*(singing)* In Amsterdam there lived a maid,
	Mark well what I do say!
	In Amsterdam there lived a maid, An' she was mistress of her trade, I'll go no more a-ro-o-vin' with you fair maid..
ALL	A-rovin', a-rovin', since rovin's bin my ru-i-in,
	I'll go no more a-rovin' with you fair maid.
BONES	One night I crept from my abode,
	Mark well what I do say!
	One night I crept from my abode, To meet this fair maid down the road. APPROACH RUBY + BOW

I'll go no more a-ro-o-vin' with you fair maid.

ALL A-rovin', a-rovin', since rovin's bin my ru-i-in,

I'll go no more a-rovin', with you fair maid.

BONES I met this fair maid after dark, *OFFER ARM*

An' took her to my favourite park.

I took this fair maid for a walk, *STAGGER*

An' we had such a lovin' talk.

ALL A-rovin', a-rovin', since rovin's bin my ru-i-in,

I'll go no more a-rovin', with you fair maid

BONES I put me arm around her waist,

RUBY Sez she, "Young man, yer in great haste!" *PUSHES AWAY*

BONES I put me hand upon her knee,

RUBY Sez she, "Young man, yer rather free!"

ALL A-rovin', a-rovin', since rovin's bin my ru-i-in,

I'll go no more a-rovin', with you fair maid

BONES We had a drink – of grub a snatch,

We sent two bottles down the hatch.

Her dainty arms was white as milk,

Her lovely hair was soft as silk.

ALL A-rovin', a-rovin', since rovin's bin my ru-i-in,

I'll go no more a-rovin', with you fair maid

BONES Her heart was poundin' like a drum,

Her lips were red as any plum.

She swore that she'd be true to me,

But she spent me money fast and free.

ALL   A-rovin', a-rovin', since rovin's bin my ru-i-in,

I'll go no more a-rovin', with you fair maid

BONES   In three weeks' time I was badly bent,

Then off to sea I sadly went.

Now when I got back home from sea,

A sailor had her on his knee.

ALL   *(finishing on a slow and deliberate finale)*

A-rovin', a-rovin', since rovin's bin my ru-i-in,

I'll go no more a-rovin', with you fair maid.

(Raucous laughter and banging of tankards upon finishing the song.)

BONES   All that singing has made my throat as dry as the Sahara Desert. More rum, Mrs Hawkins, please? Did I ever tell you you're a lovely woman?

MRS H   Flattery will get you nowhere. Alright then - just one more drink, and no more. This will be your last for today. Here, Ruby, take this to the captain.

RUBY   Here you are, sir. Your rum, sir. Better enjoy it, as it's your last!

(BONES makes a grab for RUBY, but she is too quick, and skips away laughing. Enter JW from upstage right door, who blows a short blast on her whistle.)

BONES   Not you again! Still working for aitch arrgh?

JW   Of course I am, and I have to tell you that what I have just witnessed could be interpreted as sexual harassment.

BONES   But she's a serving wench, so she's fair game.

JW   Mr Bones! That's a disgraceful attitude! Despite your
            misconstrued perception of her alleged lowly status, it is still
            a legal requirement that workers in the leisure industry
            should be accorded some respect.

BONES   Eh?

JW   *(exasperated and speaking slowly)* You... can't... molest...
            serving... wenches.

BONES   *(irritated)* Oh, go and take a walk until yer 'at floats! Yer
            beginning to annoy me!

RUBY   *(wagging her finger in his face)* So that's told you! Now
            you'll have to treat me with more respect.

BONES   *(grinning and roaring out loud)* Avast in front! Avast to
            port! Avast to starboard! *(slaps RUBY on bottom)* Avast
            behind! Aha! Arrgh!   GRAB & FAN OFF CHAIR

JW   *(getting really annoyed)* You're not listening to me. Modify
            your behaviour, or there will be consequences.

BONES   *(defiant)* Get out of it! What's the worst you can do to me?

JW   *(with a sinister smile of triumph)* I can send you on a
            Respect for Gender course in Birmingham for three weeks,
            followed by a Sexual Harassment Reappraisal in Cardiff for
            two weeks and, finally, a Behaviour Modification course in
            Milton Keynes for another week. Oh, and I forgot to
            mention, you would not be allowed to go anywhere near
            any alcohol until you had completed the full six weeks.

            *(There is a collective gasp of shock from the customers and
            BONES drops down on his knees and clasps his hands
            together to beg for mercy.)*

BONES   No! No! Not that! Anything but that! I'll behave myself, I

[handwritten: DISRESPECTFULLY]

promise! I will never speak disrespectfully to another serving
wench as long as I live! *[handwritten: REACH WITH L.H. TOWARDS HER — JW]*

JW   Neither will you touch their…rear ends.

BONES   Never. I swear.

JW   *(satisfied)* Right. But, remember, I'm watching you. *(JW
exits through upstage right door.)* *[handwritten: STAGGER TO JIM LARD — STAY STANDING]*

BONES   *(sitting back down again, looking shaken)* It's a terrible
thing…to threaten to take away a man's rum like that, lad.
Terrible. Just the thought of it has made me all of a quiver.
(He shows JIM LARD his shaking hands.) I need another
drink. *(He bawls)* Wench! *[handwritten: TURN US R TO MRS H. CHEAT SLIGHT OF JW]*

    *(JW opens the door and glares at him. Realising his mistake,
BONES affects an air of politeness.)*

    Er… Miss Ruby? Would you be so kind as to bring me
another tot of rum? I would be most grateful.

    (RUBY looks at MRS H, who is laughing.)

MRS H   Go on! Give him another rum, just for making me laugh!

    *(RUBY takes BONES a tot of rum and he elaborately
shakes her hand. JW nods and closes the door. BONES
downs the rum in one go and shudders.)*

BONES   Aagh! I needed that!

JIM LARD   You did, Mr Bones. Now… tell me about the treasure, tell
me about Captain Flint.

BONES   *(looking around and lowering his voice. All the women
pirates lean in to listen again.)* Well, Flint was a clever man.
He was never caught, you see, so he had time to hide his
treasure.

[handwritten vertical right margin: JUST L. OF CENTRE — STANDING]

JIM LARD	And you know where it was hidden?
	(The pirates lean in even closer.)
BONES	Not 'xactly, but I have a map.
JIM LARD	A treasure map?
BONES	A map of an island, Jim Lard, where Flint buried his treasure. So I know where to find the gold....but there's many a man would cut my throat for that map. *(grabbing JIM LARD by his jerkin and pulling him towards him. He whispers hoarsely)* There's one man in particular...beware of a man with one leg...Jim Lard...beware of him. He's the most evil pirate of them all. Come with me...*(he gets up, swaying, as he is now very drunk)* and I'll show you the map. Come on lad. — TAKE TANKARD OFF
	(BONES staggers out the upstage right door, followed by JIM LARD. DR. LIVESEY enters through the upstage left door. All the customers give a cheer.)
MRS H	Ah, Doctor Livesey! Is it time for your afternoon surgery, already?
LIVESEY	Yes. I suppose we'll have the usual collection of hypochondriacs and time wasters. *(He goes behind the bar, opens up his medical bag, gets out a stethoscope and a clipboard, MRS H gives him a tankard of ale.)* Most of them will want some magic medication to take away the pain, most of which is imaginary. Well, here's to the marvels of medicine. Cheers!

Song 3 – **Lily the Pink** *(assembled cast raise their tankards and start dancing)*

ALL   We'll drink a drink a drink

To Lily the Pink the Pink the Pink

The saviour of the human race

For she invented medicinal compound

Most efficacious in every case.

KATY   Mr. Frears

had sticky-out ears

and it made him awful shy

and so they gave him medicinal compound

and now he's learning how to fly.

PEARL   His brother Tony

Was notably bony

He would never eat his meals

And so they gave him medicinal compound

Now they move him round on wheels.

ALL   *4beat*   We'll drink a drink a drink

To Lily the Pink the Pink the Pink

The saviour of the human race

For she invented medicinal compound

Most efficacious in every case.

(All the customers form an orderly line in front of the bar to become the PATIENTS.)

RUBY   There's quite a lot waiting, Doctor.

LIVESEY   Well, they will all have to be patient! Patient? Get it? We'll
                    have to be quick then. No time for prolonged consultations.
                    First!

                    *(RUBY produces a small drum and stick and stands poised
                    to underscore the punch lines.)*

PATIENT 1   Doctor, Doctor. I keep thinking I'm Snow White, Donald
                    Duck or Mickey Mouse.

LIVESEY   I think you're having Disney spells.

                    (Boom, boom on drum.)

PATIENT 2   Doctor, Doctor, no one takes any notice of me.

LIVESEY   Next!

                    (Boom, boom on drum)

PATIENT 3   Doctor, Doctor. I keep singing 'The Green Green Grass of
                    Home.'

LIVESEY   Ah yes. That's what we call Tom Jones' syndrome.

PATIENT 3   Is it common?

LIVESEY   It's not unusual.

                    (Boom, boom on drum)

PATIENT 4   Doctor, I can't pronounce my Fs, Ts and Hs.

LIVESEY   Well, you can't say fairer than that. Next!

                    (Boom, boom on drum)

PATIENT 5   Doctor, I've got a strawberry in my ear.

LIVESEY   I'd better give you some cream then. *(He hands over a pot of
                    single cream.) (Boom, boom on drum)*

PATIENT 6   *(bending over, so his bottom is facing LIVESEY)* Doctor, I've got a piece of lettuce sticking out of my bum.

LIVESEY   *(leaning over the counter)* Bad news, it's the tip of an iceberg.

(Boom, boom on drum)

PATIENT 7   Doctor, Doctor, I think I'm a kleptomaniac.

LIVESEY   Are you taking anything?

(The whole cast leaps back into dance formation and resumes the song.)

ALL   We'll drink a drink a drink

To Lily the Pink the Pink the Pink

The saviour of the human race

For she invented medicinal compound

Most efficacious in every case.

MRS H   Old Ebeneezer

Thought he was Julius Caesar

And so they put him in a home

where they gave him medicinal compound

and now he's Emperor of Rome.

RUBY   Johnny Hammer

Had a terrible stammer

He could hardly say a word

And so they gave him medicinal compound

Now he's seen *(but never heard)*!

ALL   ♪   We'll drink a drink a drink

To Lily the Pink the Pink the Pink

The saviour of the human race

For she invented medicinal compound

Most efficacious in every case.

(They all scurry back into a queue in front of the bar.)

PATIENT 8	Doctor, Doctor, I feel like a billiard ball.
LIVESEY	You should be at the end of the queue.

(Boom, boom on the drum.)

PATIENT 9	Doctor, Doctor, I feel like a pack of cards.
LIVESEY	If you'll stop shuffling, I'll deal with you in a minute.

(Boom, boom on the drum.)

PATIENT 10	Doctor, Doctor, this morning I felt like a tepee. This afternoon I feel like a wigwam.
LIVESEY	You know your problem – you're two tents.

(Boom, boom on the drum.)

PATIENT 11	Doctor, do you think I need glasses?
LIVESEY	You certainly do – this is a fish and chip shop. Have your eyes ever been checked?
PATIENT 11	No, they've always been brown.

(LIVESEY gives patient some spectacles to try on)

PATIENT 11	Now I'm wearing glasses, will I be able to read?
LIVESEY	Of course.
PATIENT 11	That's funny. I never could before.

(Boom, boom on drum Next PATIENT steps up.)

LIVESEY	I have bad news. There's no other way of putting it, but you're dying. You only have ten ...

PATIENT 12   Ten what? Ten years? Ten months? Ten weeks? Ten days?

LIVESEY   No. Ten, nine, eight, seven ...

(Everyone rushes back into the dance mode and resumes singing.)

ALL   We'll drink a drink a drink

To Lily the Pink the Pink the Pink

The saviour of the human race

For she invented medicinal compound

Most efficacious in every case.

HANDBAG   Auntie Millie

Ran willy-nilly

When her legs, they did recede

And so they rubbed on medicinal compound

And now they call her Millipede.

LIVESEY   Jennifer Eccles

had terrible freckles

and the boys all called her names

but she changed with medicinal compound

and now he joins in all their games.

ALL   *12*   We'll drink a drink a drink

To Lily the Pink the Pink the Pink

The saviour of the human race

For she invented medicinal compound

Most efficacious in every case.

RUBY   Well, doctor, that's the last of your patients. But I've got a little problem myself.

LIVESEY	What seems to be the trouble?
RUBY	Well, Doctor, I've got a large pimple on the side of my face. And if you look closely, you can see some trees, a lake, and some picnic tables.
LIVESEY	Yes, it's a beauty spot.
ALL	Oooooooooooooo Weeeeeeeeeeeeeeee'll drink a drink a drink

To Lily the Pink the Pink the Pink

The saviour of the human race

For she invented medicinal compound

Most efficacious in every case.

(General merriment. Suddenly BLACK DOG bursts in through the upstage left door. Everyone stops their chatter and there is an uneasy silence.)

BLACK DOG	*(roaring)* Where's that scurvy knave Billy Bones? Come on… where is he? I know he's here. My spies tell me he's here. *(He goes up to the bar and speaks menacingly to MRS H)* Now be a good lady and go and fetch Billy Bones for me. Tell him a "friend" is asking after him.
MRS H	*(nervously)* Yes, yes, at once. Please take a seat, sir and we'll bring you over some rum. Ruby!

(MRS H motions to RUBY, who comes over. MRS H whispers in her ear and RUBY nods. BLACK DOG goes and sits at the centre stage table. RUBY brings over a tot of rum. MRS H disappears through the upstage right door and returns with BONES, who is looking anxious. JIM LARD follows.)

BONES	*(loudly)* Who is it that asks to see Billy Bones?

BLACK DOG	*(turning on his stool to face BONES)* 'Tis me, Billy lad.
BONES	*(shocked)* Black Dog! What do you want with me? Out with it man! *(He goes and sits opposite BLACK DOG at the same table.)*
BLACK DOG	We've been looking for you for some time, Billy me lad.
BONES	We?
BLACK DOG	Me and the lads who served with you aboard Flint's ship. *(He looks around)* Clever of you to hide yourself amongst all the women like this. We'd have never have found you if the drink hadn't loosened your tongue, Billy. Talk of treasure can be mighty dangerous to a man's health. *(He grabs BONES shirt and yanks him across the table.)* The map, Billy! Where's the map?
BONES	*(pulling himself free and drawing a knife)* You scurvy mongrel, Black Dog! You'll never get the map from me! You'll have to prise it from my dead, cold hands.
BLACK DOG	That can be arranged, Billy Bones. We'll come back, when you least expect us. You're a marked man now. We know where you are – and we'll be back.

(BLACK DOG stands up and strides out of the street door. BONES staggers after him, brandishing his knife.)

BONES	*(shouting out of the open door)* I'll be ready for you! I'll kill you! I'll kill you.... *(BONES collapses)*
RUBY	*(rushing over to BONES)* Oh, Mrs. Hawkins! He doesn't look very well!
MRS H	*(following RUBY)* Oh, Ruby! I think he's dead!
RUBY	I'll tell the Doctor. *(calling out)* Doctor Livesey, Mr. Billy Bones has collapsed. Will you take a look at him, please?

LIVESEY	*(coming over)* Mmm, Not a pleasant sight, and in my opinion not a pleasant smell!
MRS H	But is he dead?
LIVESEY	Good Lord, no woman. Not dead, dead drunk if you ask me.
MRS H	But what shall we do with him?
Song 4 –	**What shall we do with a drunken sailor?**
	(during the song, RUBY, JIM LARD and MRS H try valiantly to move BONES from the street doorway to the other doorway but he is a dead weight and they have great difficulty. They make a visual joke of it throughout the song. Everyone else is too busy singing to help.)
ALL	What shall we do with a drunken sailor?
	What shall we do with a drunken sailor?
	What shall we do with a drunken sailor?
	Early in the morning.
	Way-hay, up she rises,
	Way-hay, up she rises,
	Way-hay, up she rises,
	Early in the morning.
	Put him in the long boat 'til he's sober
	Put him in the long boat 'til he's sober
	Early in the morning.
	Way-hay, up she rises,
	Way-hay, up she rises,

(Handwritten annotations:) ALISON · PICK UP me (WITH STRUGGLE) · MOVE SR STILL (STAGGER) OFF STAGE AROUND STEPS

Way-hay, up she rises,

Early in the morning.

MASTER

Pull out the bung and wet him all over

Pull out the bung and wet him all over

Early in the morning.

COLLAPSE AGAIN

DS R ON EDGE OF STAGE

Way-hay, up she rises,

Way-hay, up she rises,

Way-hay, up she rises,

Early in the morning.

SUR

Put him in the scuppers with the deck pump on him

Put him in the scuppers with the deck pump on him

Early in the morning.

FAILED

ATTEMPTS

TO PICK

ME UP

Way-hay, up she rises,

Way-hay, up she rises,

Way-hay, up she rises,

Early in the morning.

GIVE UP

ATTEMPT

JIM MED

Put him in the bilge and make him drink it,

Put him in the bilge and make him drink it

Early in the morning.

Way-hay, up she rises,

Way-hay, up she rises,

Way-hay, up she rises,

Early in the morning.

Shave his belly with a rusty razor,

Shave his belly with a rusty razor,

Early in the morning.

Way-hay, up she rises,

Way-hay, up she rises,

Way-hay, up she rises,

Early in the morning.

Put 'im in bed with the Captain's daughter,

Put 'im in bed with the Captain's daughter,

Early in the morning.

Way-hay, up she rises,

Way-hay, up she rises,

Way-hay, up she rises,

Early in the morning.

MRS H	*(exhausted)* It's no good. I can't budge him any further. Oh, look, he's coming round.
BONES	Where am I?
LIVESEY	You've had a nasty turn, my man.
BONES	*(groans)* I feel like a pair of curtains.
LIVESEY	Now pull yourself together!

JIM LARD	*(to audience)* And you thought we'd finished with the doctor jokes!
BONES	What happened, where's Black Dog? *STAND*
JIM LARD	He ran off when you said you would kill him.
BONES	I will, too. Just let me catch him, that's all. — *Go upon STAGE*
LIVESEY	If you will listen to me, you horrible man. You're not to get so excited. It doesn't help.
	(They all lift BONES up and sit him on a stool at the centre stage table)
MRS H	But what's the matter with him, Doctor Livesey?
LIVESEY	I can't really say ... it must be the drink.
BONES	Well I'll see you tomorrow when you're sober then.
LIVESEY	Not me, you fool, it's you who's drunk! Mrs. Hawkins, keep him quiet, keep him still, but above all, keep him away from strong drink.
MRS H	Anything you say, Doctor Livesey! I'll do what I can to help.
LIVESEY	Well, good day to you then, Mrs Hawkins. *(LIVESEY exits through the street door.)*
BONES	Well how about some more rum, as a nightcap? That would be a great help.
MRS H	Not another drop. Drink will be the death of you. You heard what the Doctor said.
BONES	Interfering old medic. What does he know?
	(JW enters from the upstage right door and starts handing around leaflets.)
JW	I'm afraid the Doctor is quite right. Under the Government 'Drink Awareness' project, everyone is encouraged to drink

carefully. And this especially applies to you.

BONES   Not you again! Your misery is becoming infectious. I'm *very* careful with my drink. I try not to spill a drop. And I only drink for medical purposes, to 'elp me forget - forget the likes of you would be a good start!

HAVE EMPTY GLASS
& SHAKE IT

JW   I'm not going away, if that's what you think. I see it as my duty to act as your conscience.

JIM LARD   You should listen to her, Mr Bones. You don't want to die.

BONES   Everybody has to die, Jim Lard. If not to die, then perhaps tomorrow!

(JW tuts and exits through upstage right door.)

JIM LARD   I don't want you to die, as you haven't told me all about the treasure yet.

BONES   When I've had another drink, Jim Lard. You could sneak me some rum when she's not looking.

MRS H   Don't you dare, young Jim Lard. I forbid it. Take him to his room.

JIM LARD   You heard what she said, Mr. Bones.

BONES   She's a hard woman, make no mistake, Jim Lard. But I think I'll sleep here, if it's all the same to you. Near the fire, where it's warm.

MRS H   Leave him then Jim Lard. *(Ringing the ship's bell on the bar)* Come on now – everyone! Time, ladies, please! Let's have your glasses!

(Everyone groans but puts their tankards on the bar and files out of the street door, which is being held open by RUBY.)

RUBY	We'll clear away in the morning.
JIM LARD	I wouldn't be surprised if he had nightmares after all that drink!

(BONES *falls asleep in the chair. MRS H blows out the main oil lamps and the stage become dark, except for some light on the sleeping* BONES. BLACK DOG *quietly opens the door and enters the room. He is accompanied by* KATY, PEARL *and* HANDBAG.)

BLACK DOG	(whispering to the other pirates) You are going to help me find the treasure map, whilst Bones is asleep.
KATY	We'll just have a little rummage around and see if Bones has been careless.
BLACK DOG	(notices PEARL sprinkling powder from a small pouch on her belt) What are you doing Pearl?
PEARL	I'm sprinkling powder to keep the lions away.
BLACK DOG	But there aren't any lions for thousands of miles.
PEARL	I know. Strong stuff, isn't it!
BLACK DOG	Don't distract me. We're supposed to be searching.
KATY	Found anything yet, Black Dog?
BLACK DOG	Not yet, Katy.
HANDBAG	Long John won't be pleased…
BLACK DOG	I know, but Bones said nothing. He must have the map on him. He wouldn't leave it in his room.

(They *try very carefully to get at various pockets on* BONES' *jacket but he keeps mumbling and tossing and turning. Suddenly, he gives a yell in his sleep which scares them and they all run behind the bar. BONES starts talking in his sleep but he doesn't wake.)*

BONES   *(rambling in his sleep)* Fifteen men on a dead man's chest ....
            Leave me alone .... go away .... aitch arrgh .... aitch arrgh
            ...Yo ho ho and a bottle of rum ....leave me in peace.... you
            don't frighten me!

BLACK DOG   It's no good. We're not going to get anything tonight. We'll
            just have to keep a watch on him over the next few days.

            *(They creep out from behind the bar in single file and start
            the song and dance.)*

Song 5–   **We'll Be Watching You**

ALL   Every breath you take

            And every move you make

            Every bond you break

            Every step you take

            We'll be watching you

            Every single day

            And every word you say

            Every game you play

            Every night you stay

            We'll be watching you

BLACK DOG   Oh, can't you see

            The map belongs to me

            Now my poor heart aches

            With every step you take

ALL Every move you make

Every vow you break

Every smile you fake

Every claim you stake

We'll be watching you

Since the map's gone,

We've been lost without a trace

We dream at night, but can only see your face

We look around but it's the map we can't replace

We're getting old and we need to find the place,

We keep crying, treasure, treasure please!

BLACK DOG Oh, can't you see

The map belongs to me

Now my poor heart aches

Every step you take

Every move you make

Every vow you break

Every smile you fake

Every claim you stake

We'll be watching you

(They start to move slowly, in rhythm, towards and out of the street door.)

Every move you make

Every step you take

We'll be watching you

We'll be watching you

Every breath you take

Every move you make

Every bond you break

Every step you take

(We'll be watching you)

Every single day

Every word you say

Every game you play

Every night you stay

(We'll be watching you)

Every move you make

Every vow you break

Every smile you fake

Every claim you stake

(We'll be watching you)

Every single day

Every word you say

Every game you play

Every night you stay

(They poke their heads around the door to deliver the final line)

(WE'LL BE WATCHING YOU.)

Fade music and lights. BLACKOUT.

END OF SCENE

TREASURE ISLAND
ACT 1.
SCENE 2

The Admiral Benbow, next morning. All the usual customers are there –
carousing with their tankards. BONES is still asleep, slumped over his table.
MRS H, RUBY and JIM LARD are serving from behind the bar.

Song. 6–	**Wild Rover**
ALL	I've been a wild rover for many's the year
	I've spent all me money on whiskey and beer
	But now I'm returning with gold in great store
	And I never will play the wild rover no more
	And it's no, nay, never,
	No, nay never no more
	Will I play the wild rover,
	No never no more
	I went in to an alehouse I used to frequent
	And I told the landlady me money was spent
	I asked her for credit, she answered me nay
	Such a custom as you I can have any day
	(JW bursts in through the upstage right door, shouting and
	waving her arms.)
JW	Stop! Stop! All this constant talk of drinking should not be
	allowed! I will remind you all of the Government directive

to drink sensibly and in moderation!

ALL   *(shout)* Shut up, you silly woman!

(JW staggers back in astonishment. RUBY hands her a tot of rum, which JW downs without thinking, then she disappears through the door again. The song continues.)

ALL   And it's no, nay, never,

No, nay never no more

Will I play the wild rover,

No never no more

KATY   I took up from my pocket, ten sovereigns bright

And the landlady's eyes opened wide with delight

She says "I have whiskeys and wines of the best

And the words that I told you were only in jest."

ALL   And it's no, nay, never,

No, nay never no more

Will I play the wild rover,

No never no more

PEARL   I'll go home to my parents, confess what I've done

And I'll ask them to pardon their prodigal son

And, when they've caressed me as oft times before

I never will play the wild rover no more

ALL   And it's no, nay, never,

No, nay never no more

Will I play the wild rover,

No never no more.

(General merriment. BONES wakes up and staggers to the bar.)

GO TO INSIDE EDGE OF BAR (L)

BONES   I've a bit of a thick 'ead this morning, Ruby.

RUBY   I'm not surprised after what happened yesterday.

BONES   I had a funny dream last night. But I can't remember much about yesterday.

RUBY   You tried to kill Black Dog!

BONES   And I will too, if I get the chance!

JIM LARD   Why are you so frightened of Black Dog?

BONES   It's his friends who worry me more than he does. I'm not afraid of him!

JIM LARD   Better take things easy today.

BONES   I'll be fine when I've had another drink.

JIM LARD   But you know what the Doctor said.

BONES   What does he know, interfering old medic. *(Pounding on the bar and shouting)* Some more rum! A bottle this time, or I'll slit your throat from ear to ear!

JIM LARD   Here you are! *(He hands over a bottle to BONES)*

BONES   And something to eat – I'd like a sandwich if it's not too much trouble.

(JIM LARD produces a golf club from under the bar.)

BONES   What's this?

LEAVE DRINK ON BAR – MOVE DS C

JIM LARD   Sorry. I thought you asked for a sand wedge. Now tell me some _more_ about Captain Flint.

KEEP SAND WEDGE — USE AS PROP — STAGGER

BONES   An evil, wicked man was Flint. His skin was all wrinkled, and he was a mean man. The crew used to call him 'Old Skin' Flint, but never to his face.

JIM LARD   He sounds horrible. But what about his treasure?

(All the customers stop talking and lean towards BONES to try and hear the conversation.)

BONES   Buried on a deserted island, it was. And, as I told you, I have the map!

STAY BY BAR

JIM LARD   Where do you keep it?

(Everyone leans in a little closer.)

BONES   Better that you don't know.

(Suddenly, a rhythmic tapping sound is heard from outside. All the customers gasp.)

BONES   I know that sound! Don't tell him I'm here! Don't let him near me!

JIM LARD   But who is it, and why are you so frightened?

BONES   It's Pew, Blind Pew!

RUN ROUND & HIDE BEHIND Jim

(The customers all scream.)

KATY   It's Blind Pew!

PEARL   Blind Pew!

HANDBAG   Quick, hide!

(Everyone, except JIM LARD and BONES, rushes behind the bar and ducks down, then bobs back up so that the audience can just see their eyes and the top of their heads.)

HIDE BEHIND Jim ← → RH SIDE
— SIT B/ TABLE

JIM LARD:

I'll send him away. Leave him to me!

(BLIND PEW flings open the street door. He is dressed in a long black cloak, wears dark glasses, a big hat and carries a white stick, which he taps on the ground.)

BLIND PEW

Is there anyone there?

JIM LARD

(going up to BLIND PEW) What do you want? There's no one here but me.

BLIND PEW

Give me your hand. You've got a kind voice. Help an old blind beggar.

(JIM LARD holds out his hand, which Blind Pew grabs and twists JIM's arm round his back.)

JIM LARD

Ouch! Let go! You're hurting me! Get off!

BLIND PEW

(in a nasty voice) Take me to Billy Bones!

JIM LARD

He's not here. Ouch! alright!

BLIND PEW

Of course he's here! I can smell him! No-one stinks of rum like Billy Bones.

BONES

Pew, Pew!

(Everyone behind the bar, bobs up slightly and says "Barney McGrew, Cuthbert, Dibble and Grubb." Then they bob back down again. BLIND PEW propels JIM LARD towards BONES and then lets JIM go.)

BLIND PEW

Give me your hand, Billy Bones. *(BONES holds out his hand and BLIND PEW puts something in it. There the message is delivered.)*

BONES

(horrified) No, no! Take it back! Pew...Pew...

(Everyone behind the bar, bobs up slightly and says "Barney McGrew, Cuthbert, Dibble and Grubb." Then they bob

back down again. BLIND PEW walks towards the street door, tapping his stick and then he turns.)

BLIND PEW   You have until ten tonight. *(BLIND PEW laughs horribly and then leaves.)*

BONES   *(unfolds a large, many times folded piece of paper/material to reveal an enormous black spot)* The black spot, the black spot! He's given me the black spot!

(Everyone behind the bar stands up and gasps. Then they all rush out of the tavern, leaving only MRS H, RUBY, JIM LARD and BONES.)

JIM LARD   *(he takes black spot paper/material and lays it on the table like a tablecloth)* O.K. We get the picture. You've got the black spot. But what is it? What does it mean?

BONES   It means I'm a dead man. It means they're coming for me! I need another drink! I'll kill that blind beggar Pew. *(Picks up sand wedge and flails around him, then collapses)*

JIM LARD   Mother! Mother! Mr Bones has collapsed!

MRS H   Fetch the Doctor, Ruby.

(RUBY rushes out.)

JIM LARD   I think it's too late this time. He's dead!

MRS H   And he still owes us money!

JIM LARD   There might be some in his pocket.

MRS H   *(searches his pockets, finds some coins)* I'll only take what I'm owed.

JIM LARD   Help me find the map!

MRS H   What map?

JIM LARD	I'll explain later, the pirates will be here very soon. We need to find a key! *(searching BONES frantically)* There's one on a string round his neck.
MRS H	Try it in his chest!
JIM LARD	*(trying the key through BONES' shirt)* There isn't a keyhole!
MRS H	Not his chest chest, Jim! The other one! The sea chest! In his room!
JIM LARD	Yes, of course! I'll be right back!
BLACK DOG	*(offstage)* Come on men! He's in there, with his treasure map! Let's get him!
	(There is a shot offstage, followed by men's voices shouting to each other. Mrs H screams and runs to hide behind the bar.)
SQUIRE	*(offstage)* The blind man's dead! The rest of you had better come out or you'll be next!
BLACK DOG	*(offstage)* Curse you – you interfering landlubber!
	(Another couple of shots are heard, followed by a yell from one of the pirates.)
LIVESEY	*(offstage)* I think I wounded another one, Squire!
SQUIRE	*(offstage)* They're making a run for it, Livesey! I think we've routed them!
	(JIM LARD appears from the upstage right door, clutching a map. The SQUIRE, LIVESEY and RUBY come through the street door. The two men are brandishing pistols.)
LIVESEY	Ah, Jim! Is your mother alright?
MRS H	*(popping up from behind the bar)* Yes I'm fine, Squire Pegg. Thank goodness you got here in time!

LIVESEY	I see Billy Bones is dead. Did the pirates get him?
MRS H	No, doctor. He died from the drink, just as you said he would.
JIM LARD	They were after his treasure map. This one. I found it in his sea chest. Can we try to find the treasure, sir? Can we?
SQUIRE	Most certainly. Treasure hunting sounds so exciting, if we can find the island.
RUBY	I overheard Mr Bones talking once. Dead Man's Chest is the name of the island.
	(JIM LARD opens the map out and lays it on the table. Everyone crowds round to look at it.)
SQUIRE	From my geography lessons at school, I seem to recall that Dead Man's Chest is in the Virgin Islands, so at least we know roughly where to start.
LIVESEY	There will be dangers. We know there will be others who want the map.
JIM LARD	Those pirates will stop at nothing.
SQUIRE	I think it a good idea, Jim Lard, if the Doctor and I move into this tavern to keep an eye on you all. But first we must go in search of a ship. I have friends in Falmouth. They know a thing or two about sailing.
JIM LARD	Then we really are going to sail? We're going to search for Flint's treasure?
LIVESEY	Just as soon as we can hire a ship.
SQUIRE	But we will still need a crew to sail the ship. None of my men are seafaring men.
LIVESEY	If they agree, Mrs Hawkins and Ruby can accompany us on

the voyage. I don't see why they shouldn't come. There'll be lots of washing, cleaning and ironing to do.

MRS H   Careful! Don't you take anything for granted. We're liberated women, aren't we Ruby?

RUBY   The last man who mentioned washing and ironing to me got a busted nose!

MRS H   And if you didn't make a mess, there would be no need for cleaning too.

RUBY   So just watch it, that's all.

SQUIRE   Point taken. If you come with us, you'll be treated as equals.

MRS H   Equals? That's a step down for a start!

LIVESEY   To Falmouth then, to hire a ship and a captain to take us to Treasure Island! Then we shall advertise for a crew and hold interviews here in the Admiral Benbow.

JIM LARD   Treasure! Treasure Island! I'm going to be rich!

MRS H   No, Jim. We're all going to be rich! I can see it now!

RUBY   Money, money and more money!

Song 7–   **Money, Money, Money.**

ALL   Money, money, money

           Must be funny

           In the rich man's world

           Money, money, money

           Always sunny

           In the rich man's world

Aha-ahaaa

All the things I could do

If I had a little money

It's a rich man's world

RUBY   I work all night, I work all day,

                to pay the bills I have to pay

ALL   Ain't it sad

RUBY   And still there never seems to be

                a single penny left for me

ALL   That's too bad

RUBY   In my dreams I have a plan

                If I got me a wealthy man

                I wouldn't have to work at all,

                I'd fool around and have a ball...

ALL   Money, money, money

                Must be funny

                In the rich man's world

                Money, money, money

                Always sunny

                In the rich man's world

                Aha-ahaaa

All the things I could do

If I had a little money

It's a rich man's world

MRS H   A man like that is hard to find

but I can't get him off my mind

ALL   Ain't it sad

MRS H   And if he happens to be free

I bet he wouldn't fancy me

ALL   That's too bad

GET UP EXIT US C

MRS H   So I must leave, I'll have to go

To Las Vegas or Monaco

And win a fortune in a game,

my life will never be the same

LIVESEY   *(interrupting)* If I can just add a note of caution. No one, I repeat no one, must mention the real purpose of our voyage. We must keep our secret.

SQUIRE   The Doctor is quite right. It wouldn't be safe if the real reason for our voyage was discovered.

MRS H   We could say that we are entering the Whitbread Round the World Race ....

RUBY   .... and we could lose our way when we get near to the island.

SQUIRE   An excellent subterfuge! You're not just a pretty face, Ruby!

LIVESEY: To Falmouth then, to hire a ship!

ALL   *(resuming song)*

                Money, money, money

                Must be funny

                In the rich man's world

                Money, money, money

                Always sunny

                In the rich man's world

                Aha-ahaaa

                All the things I could do

                If I had a little money

                It's a rich man's world

                        REPEAT LAST LINE

BLACKOUT.

END OF SCENE

TREASURE ISLAND

ACT 1.

SCENE 3.

The Admiral Benbow Inn again. There is a large sign on the bar which says "Crew Wanted for Round The World Voyage". All the regular customers are assembled there, plus LONG JOHN SILVER who has a wooden leg, a hook for a hand and an eye patch. MRS H, RUBY and JIM LARD are behind the bar serving. Everyone is singing, as the lights go up.

Song 8–	**Blow the man down.**
ALL	Oh! Blow the man down, bullies. Blow the man down.
	Way! Hey! Blow the man down!
	Oh! Blow the man down bullies. Blow him right down.
	Give us ~~the~~ *some* time ~~and we'll~~ *to* blow the man down!
SILVER	As I was a-walking down Paradise Street,
ALL	Way! Hey! Blow the man down!
SILVER	A pretty young damsel I wanted to meet,
ALL	Walked with a man, oh blow the man down.
SILVER	I says to her, "Polly, and how d'ye do?"
ALL	Way ay! Blow the man down!
SILVER	She says, "None the better for seeing of you!"
ALL	Oh gimme some time to blow the man down.
ALL	Oh we'll blow the man up and we'll blow the man down,

Way ay! Blow the man down!

We'll blow him away into Liverpool Town,

Oh gimme some time to blow the man down.

SILVER   I swung to the left and swung to the right,

ALL   Way! Hey! Blow the man down!

SILVER   But he was a guy who sure knew how to fight,

ALL   None of his blows could blow the man down.

SILVER   All ye sailors take warning before you set sail,

ALL   Way! Hey! Blow the man down!

SILVER   If he's strong as an ox and big as a whale,

ALL   Think twice before you blow the man down.

ALL   Come all ye young fellers that follows the sea.

                Way! Hey! Blow the man down!

                I'll sing ye a song if ye'll listen to me.

                Give us the time and we'll blow the man down!

                *(LIVESEY, THE SQUIRE and CAPT. SMOLLETT enter
                from the upstage right door.)*

LIVESEY   Mrs Hawkins, may I introduce our Captain, Captain
                Smollett?

MRS H   Delighted to make your acquaintance, Captain Smollett.

LIVESEY: Smollett is an old friend of the family. I would trust him
                with my wife.

MRS H   Your wife, don't you mean your life?

LIVESEY	I don't know whether I would trust him that far!
SMOLLETT	Gentlemen! And ladies, of course. If we can be serious. Searching for treasure is no matter of frivolity!
	(The pirates all look at each other, nudge and wink at the sound of the word "treasure.")
SQUIRE	*(in an alarmed whisper)* Keep your voice down! I thought we had a secret?
SMOLLETT	It's no secret round these parts.
LIVESEY:	We must be on our guard.
SQUIRE	Now what about a ship?
LIVESEY	I saw one called the 'Polo'. I thought she was in mint condition – but she was unseaworthy. She had a hole in the middle!
SMOLLETT	But I have found one called the 'Black Pig'. Used to belong to a Captain Pugwash, but for our voyage she will be renamed the 'Hispaniola'.
LIVESEY:	And when can we take charge?
SMOLLETT	Immediately.
LIVESEY	But we have to choose a crew.
SQUIRE	Well, Mrs Hawkins has advertised for a crew *(he indicates the sign)* and this is why the place is so full today. That man over there *(he points to SILVER)* was once a sea cook. He's assembled us a potential crew, and he'll come along himself too.
	(SILVER is leaning against the bar, surrounded by pirates.)
SILVER	... and then he asked me how I lost my leg. Told 'im it was taken away by a cannonball. And I lost my 'and when I was

swept overboard by a giant wave, and a shark bit my 'and orff! Then he asked about my eye! Told him that a seagull pooped in it. So 'e says, 'But that shouldn't mean you lost an eye', and I said 'Well, it was me first day with me 'ook!'

(Pirates all fall about laughing)

SMOLLETT	*(shouts)* Mr Silver? A moment of your time please!
SILVER	*(going over to SMOLLETT)* Pleased to be of assistance, kind sirs.
LIVESEY	But this man has a pronounced limp.
JIM LARD:	*(to audience)* L. I. M. P. pronounced limp!
SILVER	Oh, that was really funny young man. Allow me to introduce myself, gentlemen. Silver's the name, though I have a heart of gold! Just my little jest, sirs!
LIVESEY	I cannot see how a man with one leg can help us.
SILVER	I'll be right upset if you turn me down. In fact I'll be hopping mad!
SMOLLETT	I don't know if we can put up with your sense of humour.
LIVESEY	We may be able to tolerate you if you can help find a crew.
SILVER	A crew for the Whitbread Race was it? No problem. All my friends are sailors!

(Pirates all snigger in background)

LIVESEY	Ah, yes. The Whitbread Race.
SILVER	If I'd only got one arm, I could enter the race single handed!
SQUIRE	Really, this is too much!
SILVER	Begging your pardon, Sirs. Katy, Pearl, Handbag, come 'ere.
SMOLLETT	But these are all women!

KATY	He's observant, I'll give him that.
PEARL	Yeah. I like a captain who knows what's what.
SILVER	Begging your pardon, sir, but I always works with female pirates.
SQUIRE	Why is that?
SILVER	Have you not heard, sir? The female of the species is deadlier than the male. *(SILVER puts his arm around KATY's shoulders.)*

Song 9–   **The Female of the Species is Deadlier than the Male.**

SILVER   She whispers oh such pretty lies

Don't believe her

For when you look into her eyes

Love just isn't there

ALL WOMEN   Brother, beware

Take care, my brother, take care

For the female of the species is deadlier than the male

(SILVER moves on to put his arm around PEARL)

SILVER   The smile that made a dream begin

Clouds your vision

It's just the shadow of a dream

That you're living in

ALL WOMEN   She never cared

Beware, my brother, beware

For the female of the species is deadlier than the male

(SILVER moves on to put his arm around HANDBAG)

SILVER   Memories of kisses on a summer's day

That's all she left you when she went away

Now, you pay!

By walking streets, you'll never know

When the night comes

Sitting at places that you go

Hoping she'll be there

ALL WOMEN   Brother, beware

Take care, my brother, take care

For the female of the species is deadlier than the male

(HANDBAG leers at SMOLLETT and draws a dagger with which she strokes his face. He looks unnerved.)

SMOLLETT   Yes...well...I take your point. How do you...er...you ladies...feel about joining the Whitbread Race?

KATY   The Whitbread Race?

PEARL   Round the World?

HANDBAG   No way! We're not interested! You must be joking!

PEARL   Much too dangerous!

SILVER   *(hastily)* Just let me have a quiet word, gentlemen. *(he takes the women to one side and whispers)* Captain Flint .... Treasure .... need I say more?

ALL WOMEN   *(together to SMOLLETT)* Fine!

KATY   Excellent idea!

PEARL   When do we start?

SQUIRE   We sail on the morning tide.

               (Enter JW from upstage right door, brandishing forms)

JW   Wait a minute! Wait a minute!

               (Everyone groans)

               You can't just employ someone like that! What about job
               assessments, safety assessments and contracts?

SQUIRE   Well...er...I hadn't thought...

JW   Exactly! You hadn't thought. It's a good job I'm here to
               make sure that everything is done shipshape and Bristol
               fashion. Contracts of employment. *(She hands them out to
               SILVER and the pirates)* Job assessment forms and safety
               assessment forms. *(She hands those to SMOLLETT)* And
               don't even think about setting sail until those forms are
               completed.

SMOLLETT   But I've never filled in forms like this in all my years at sea!

JW   It's clear from your attitude that you don't take employees
               rights and health and safety very seriously. *(Bitterly)*
               Everywhere I go, I'm met with hostility or indifference. *(She
               begins to get tearful)*

SILVER   Now, now. Don't take on so. *(He produces a filthy
               handkerchief and passes it to her. She views it with horror.)*
               You have us at a disadvantage. You're talking about our
               responsibilities to keep not only ourselves but everyone else
               safe, and no one has ever explained to us in simple language
               what we can all do to minimise risk.

JW   This is remarkably positive of you, Mr Silver. I'm encouraged.

SILVER	Well, me and the ladies are all agreed that what we needs is a training day.
JW	A training day?
SILVER	That's it! A day when we can do some team building. Where we can improve our interpersonal skills. You could introduce some individual development targets, and we could 'ave an annual appraisal when we could see if we had achieved our objectives.
JW	This is wonderful! I usually meet with such hostility. I'll go and plan the arrangements immediately. Oh, Mr Silver! You have gone up in my estimation.
SILVER	Aargh! Thank you ma'am.
	(JW disappears through upstage right door.)
	(To SMOLLETT) That should keep the old biddy happy for a while. By the time she's got a training day programme planned, we'll be halfway to the Cape of Good Hope!
	(Everyone laughs)
LIVESEY	By Jove, Squire Pegg! I think this chap may be pretty useful after all!
SQUIRE	I think you're right, Livesey!
SMOLLETT	I feel that I should interview some of the crew, however. *(to KATY)* Morgan, what did you do before going to sea?
KATY	I was a human cannonball sir.
SILVER	But she was fired!
PEARL	Women of her calibre are hard to find!
SMOLLETT	And what about you, Pretty Pearl Plank? I suppose you've got a funny line too?

PEARL	With a name like Plank, I seem to have been on board all me life!
SMOLLETT	And what about you Handbag Jones?
HANDBAG	Bag's my choice of weapon and bag's my chosen disposition.
SILVER	As in "old bag", you understand sir. Ow! *(HANDBAG whacks him with her bag)*
SQUIRE	Are you sure we haven't hired a crew of comedians?
LIVESEY	In recognition of your help, Silver, you can be Captain Smollett's First Mate.
SILVER	*(putting his arm through SMOLLETT's and giving him an evil smile)* And right friendly I'll be sir, if you know what I mean.
SMOLLETT	*(hastily unhooking his arm)* Now what about some more to make up the rest of the crew?
SILVER	None of my crew wears make-up, sir.
LIVESEY	But you can find more if we need them?
SILVER	You leave everything to me. Worry no more. I'll supply a crew the likes of which you've never seen before. Sailors ready to grasp this ... er ...golden opportunity.
JIM LARD	*(raising his hand)* Ooh! Me! Me! I want to be cabin boy!
SILVER	*(going over to JIM)* And who might you be, young feller me lad?
JIM LARD	Jim Lard, at your service, Mr Silver.
SILVER	We I reckon you look like a fine, strong specimen. Welcome aboard Jim Lard.
JIM LARD	Thank you Mr.Silver.

SILVER	Nay, lad. I feel you and I are going to be good mates. Call me Long John, like the rest of me mates do.
JIM LARD	Thank you Long John.
SMOLLETT	Fine. Everything settled. We sail on tomorrow's tide.

Song. 10–   **Sailing.**

(Everyone on stage does synchronised swaying)

ALL   We are sailing, We are sailing, home again 'cross the sea.

We are sailing, stormy waters, to be near you, to be free.

We are flying, We are flying, like a bird 'cross the sky.

We are flying, passing high clouds, to be with you, to be free.

Can you hear us, can you hear us, thro' the dark night, far away,

We are dying, forever trying, to be with you, who can say.

Can you hear us, can you hear us, thro' the dark night far away.

We are dying, forever trying, to be with you, who can say.

We are sailing, we are sailing, home again 'cross the sea.

We are sailing stormy waters, to be near you, to be free.

Oh Lord, to be near you, to be free.

Oh Lord, to be near you, to be free, Oh Lord.

BLACKOUT.

END OF ACT 1.

TREASURE ISLAND

ACT II.

SCENE 1.

On board the Hispaniola. (SEE SET PLAN 2) The backcloth is just sky, with some clouds. On the stage is a ship's wheel, various large barrels dotted about (one needs to open at the top for JW to appear from and JIM to climb into later). Side flats show the side of the captain's cabin and some rigging. Other ship's items can be dotted about as set dressing. All the pirates are on stage, plus MRS H and RUBY. Everyone is assisting in bringing supplies etc. on board. MRS H is carrying a basket filled with cleaning materials and other bits. RUBY is checking off items on a clipboard. JW is hidden in the apple barrel.

Song 10–	Reprise – Sailing
	(all the crew doing synchronised swaying)
ALL	We are sailing, we are sailing, home again 'cross the sea.
	We are sailing, stormy waters, to be near you, to be free.
	We are flying, we are flying, like a bird 'cross the sky.
	We are flying, passing high clouds, to be with you, to be free.
	Can you hear us, can you hear us, thro' the dark night, far away,
	We are dying, forever trying, to be with you, who can say.

Can you hear us, can you hear us, thro' the dark night far
away.

We are dying, forever trying, to be with you, who can say.

We are sailing, we are sailing, home again 'cross the sea.
We are sailing stormy waters, to be near you, to be free.

Oh Lord, to be near you, to be free. Oh Lord, to be near
you, to be free, Oh Lord.

SILVER   *(to audience)* I think I should summarise where we've got to.
              Jim Lard has Flint's map, and along with the Captain, the
              Doctor and the Squire they have commissioned this ship.
              With my assistance, they have a crew, but what they don't
              know is that most of them are bloodthirsty pirates. It don't
              matter that they are female! Everybody knows that when it
              comes to conniving, the female of the species is far deadlier
              than the male. When the time comes, we'll take the ship, and
              take the treasure too. Now look out, here comes the
              Captain.

              (SMOLLETT enters from the "cabin")

SMOLLETT   We're almost ready!

MRS H   It's so good of you to let me and Ruby come along. We can
              both keep an eye on young Jim.

SMOLLETT   Remember, your role is to keep the ship spic and span. Ruby
              will help with the cleaning. I'm a real stickler that the ship
              should be as clean and hygienic as possible. Disease has been
              the downfall of many a badly planned voyage.

RUBY   I've remembered the pickled cabbage, and there's a large barrel of fresh apples so the crew can get their daily dose of vitamins.

LIVESEY: Now, is everybody safely on board?

SMOLLETT   Weigh the anchor!

ALL   Two tons sir!

SILVER   At least you two ladies do not need to worry about the cooking in the galley. That's all in hand.

MRS H   Just look at your 'ook, Mr Silver. It's starting to go rusty. Get some of that in the food and we'll all have food poisoning. *(She sprays the 'ook with disinfectant and gives it a good polish.)*

RUBY   And look at Long John's long johns! When did you last change them?

SILVER   Change them? Did you think I had another pair?

MRS H   Take these, *(she produces a pair of pink long johns from her basket)* and next time you undress, change them. I'm sorry they're pink, but the colours ran in the wash.

SILVER   I don't reckon to undress much either. You ladies have a peculiar idea of life on board ship. It's not like being at 'ome. It's not as if I'm a squire, or anything.

                (JW suddenly pops out of a barrel.)

JW   Captain Smollett? I need to explain about some of my expectations.

SILVER   *(bellowing)* Stowaway!

SMOLLETT   What on earth are you doing on board my ship?

JW   You know who I am? *(extending her hand)* Hermione

Jobsworth at your service.

SMOLLETT   *(shaking her hand)* I believe we have met, madam. But I need you to remember that this is my ship, and I take full responsibility for all eventualities on board. You can make observations. Indeed, you can make recommendations. But I must insist that whatever you say is categorised as advice. And the beauty of advice is that it can be ignored.

JW   Nevertheless, there are things that must be said. I have the following conditions before I consider this to be a safe project. All sailors working below decks have to wear safety helmets. Head height does not conform to building regulations, and there is serious risk of head injury. Secondly, all sailors working at height need to have safety nets.

SMOLLETT   Safety nets? This isn't a circus, you know.

JW   Third on my list – all sailors working in noisy areas will need to wear ear protection. This particularly applies to those working on the gun deck. Finally, for the moment, all sailors need to take an eye test, to see if any of them need to wear glasses. I have here a chart for all the pirates when they take an eye test.

(She produces a chart which reads:

R

R R H R R

R R H R H R R

R O R R O R H R O R R O R)

Perhaps Mr Silver could read it through for us?

SILVER   If I must! Got to keep her sweet, if you know what I mean.

                  (JW, still in the barrel, holds up the chart, whilst SILVER
                  produces a telescope and reads it from a distance.)

SILVER   Aargh, aargh, aargh, haitch, aargh, aargh, aargh, aargh,
                  haitch, aargh, haitch, aargh, aargh, aargh, ho, aargh, aargh,
                  ho, aargh, haitch, aargh, ho, aargh, aargh, aargh, ho, aargh.
                  Reminds me of a song I used to sing when I was drunk!

JW   Very good Mr Silver. Considering you only have one eye.
                  Now, I also have warning sign to display on the deck,
                  especially after rain, or a heavy storm. *(She produces a*
                  sign from the barrel which says 'WET FLOOR' in large
                  letters) – and, gentlemen, this is not an instruction!

SMOLLETT   I'll certainly consider your suggestions. Thank you for your
                  interest.

                  (JW nods, climbs out of the barrel and then starts an
                  inspection of the crew, writing notes in a little book.)

SILVER   *(going up to SMOLLETT and speaking confidentially)* I
                  'ope, cap'n, that you're not going to take too much notice of
                  'er. She's had a go at everybody so far, so there's no reason
                  why she should leave you out. She's never 'appy unless she's
                  making everyone else miserable. But let's keep a 'ealthy
                  perspective on things aboard this ship. Eh?

SMOLLETT   I hear you, Silver.

                  (MRS HAWKINS and RUBY start rigging up a washing line
                  which stretches right across the stage)

MRS H   Now ladies! You've seen how the men are on this ship. And
                  it's no surprise to us. They're lazy and untidy. They don't

put anything away. Put things down, yes. But then they just leave them. They don't wash very often either so we've a lot to put right? And we can start right now, here on the deck. We'll get this sorted, and leave below deck for another day.

Song 11.–   **Sisters are doing it for themselves.**

(Mrs H, RUBY, JW and female pirates perform a dance routine with mops and buckets, whilst hanging out some washing.)

ALL   Now, there was a time

when they used to say

that behind ev'ry great man,

there had to be a great woman.

But oh, in these times of change,

you know that it's no longer true.

So we're comin' out of the kitchen,

'cause there's something we forgot to say to you.

We say, Sisters are doin' it for themselves,

standin' on their own two feet

and ringin' on their own bells.

We say, Sisters are doin' it

for themselves.

Now, this is a song to celebrate

the conscious liberation of the female state.

Mothers, daughters,

and their daughters too, woah, yeah,

woman to woman,

we're singing with you, ooh, ooh.

The "inferior sex" has got a new exterior.

We got doctors, lawyers, politicians too,

ooh, ooh, ooh, ooh.

Ev'rybody, take a look around.

Can you see, can you see, can you see,

there's a woman right next to yo-ou.

We say, Sisters are doin' it for themselves,

standin' on their own two feet

and ringin' on their own bells.

Sisters are doin' it

for themselves.

There was a time,

oh, when they used to say

that behind ev'ry great man,

there had to be a great woman.

In these times of change,

you know that it's no longer true.

So we're comin' out of the kitchen,

'cause there's something we forgot to say to you.

We say, Sisters are doin' it for themselves,

standin' on their own two feet

and ringin' on their own bells.

Sisters are doin' it

for themselves.

Sisters are doin' it

for themselves.

(SQUIRE, LIVESEY and JIM LARD enter from "cabin". The pirates gather in a group around SILVER and look miserable.)

SMOLLETT   *(looks at washing line through telescope)* I don't understand that message. It seems to say "Dinner at seven 'o'clock"!

SQUIRE   That's not a message, Captain. It's Mrs Hawkins' washing.

SMOLLETT   I thought I hadn't seen those flags before.

SQUIRE   I don't like the mood of the crew, captain. They seem ugly.

SMOLLETT   Don't be silly, they always look like that.

LIVESEY   I think the Squire is right. They talk in very low voices, and stop if you get within earshot.

SQUIRE   Are you sure they know nothing of the real reason for our voyage?

LIVESEY   I hope it is still a secret. If not, we might be in trouble. Some of the crew look familiar to me. They might have been with the bunch we shot at outside the Admiral Benbow Inn and, if I'm right, they know about the treasure. I wish we could be certain.

JIM LARD	They seem to trust me. I'll see what I can find out.
SQUIRE	Well, you be careful Jim Lard. These are dangerous men.
LIVESEY	Silver definitely seems to be their leader.
SMOLLETT	I don't think they will try anything until we reach the island.
SQUIRE	We must secure the guns and provisions in the hold.
LIVESEY	Jim Lard, you keep an eye on the crew.
	(SMOLLETT, SQUIRE and LIVESEY exit to "cabin")
JIM LARD	I think I'll have an apple whilst I'm waiting. There's not many left. I'll have to climb in.
	(JIM climbs in the barrel. He bobs up with one in his hand but then bobs back down again when SILVER and the pirates stroll over towards the barrel.)
KATY	I say we strike now!
SILVER	Not yet! Let them sail to the island first. They've got the map after all. Be patient.
KATY	Patience is a card game. Patience is for wimps. I can't wait much longer.
PEARL	It's time we let them know what's what.
HANDBAG	We've had no action for ages.
SILVER	I'm telling you, you've got to bide your time. Wait for the moment, that's all I ask.
KATY	Squire Pegg is mine when we do strike. I 'ate that man! I'll wring his neck and throw him down the hold.
SILVER	It will not work! You cannot fit Squire Pegg into a round hold!
HANDBAG	Only the four of us know the plan.

SILVER	And that's how it must stay. Not a word to anyone. Let this be our little secret!
	(SILVER and the pirates exit stage right. JIM LARD bobs up out of the barrel.)
JIM LARD	I must warn the Captain! *(He runs to the "cabin" entrance and calls out.)* Captain! Squire! Doctor! Come quickly!
	(SMOLLETT, SQUIRE and LIVESEY appear.)
	They're going to mutiny! I heard them plotting!
SQUIRE	Who was there, Jim Lard?
JIM LARD	Well, Silver was there, and Morgan, and the other might have been Plank. I couldn't see, but I could hear. I had to keep out of sight. If they had seen me, I don't know what would have happened.
LIVESEY	What did you hear, Jim Lard?
JIM LARD	They will wait until we reach the island, and then attack.
SMOLLETT	Then we must surprise them. When we reach the island we will let them go ashore. That way we keep control of the ship.
SQUIRE	A safe position, considering we're outnumbered.
PEARL	Land Ahoy! Land Ahoy!
SMOLLETT	Gather round men...er... women. I propose to let you go ashore to collect fruit and fresh water.
SILVER	That's a mighty fine gesture, captain, for a man to make to his loyal crew. Three cheers for the captain. Hip, hip ... oh, never mind. Please yourselves.
SMOLLETT	Lower the boat!

Song 12–   **Row, row, row the boat**

(With much audience participation, words on display etc.
All verses sung. Next, pirates divide the audience so song
can be sung as a round, in competition, using only the first
three verses.)

Row, row, row the boat

Gently down the stream

Merrily merrily merrily merrily

Life is but a dream.

Row, row, row the boat

Gently as can be

Cause if you're not careful

You'll fall into the sea!

Row, row, row your boat

Gently down the lake

Don't stand up and rock the boat

That's a big mistake!

Row, row, row the boat

Gently down the stream

If you see a crocodile

Don't forget to scream.

Row, row, row the boat

Gently down the river

If you see a polar bear

Don't forget to shiver.

3   Row, row, row the boat

Gently to the shore

If you see a hungry lion

Don't forget to roar

Row, row, row the boat

There's a spider in the bath.

And when your mummy screams out loud

Don't forget to laugh.

4   Row, row, row your boat

Across the ocean blue.

And if we find some treasure there

We'll not share it with you.

SILVER   If it's all the same with you, sir, we'll leave some crew
behind to help you. We wouldn't want anything to happen
to the ship now, would we?

(Most pirates leave, but two remain)

LIVESEY   *(To the SQUIRE)* I think we had better alter our plans.
According to the map, there's a stockade on the island –
we'd be much safer there.

SQUIRE   *(drawing his pistol)* You two! Put up your hands, and walk
slowly over to the hold.

(The pirates do as they're told)

Now climb down! Lock it securely, Jim Lard!

LIVESEY   Mrs Hawkins, we need someone to guard these villains even though they're locked into the hold.

MRS H   Why, Ruby and I could do that. It would leave you men free to do what needs to be done on the island.

RUBY   Just give me a pistol, and I'll make sure that they stay where they are.

SMOLLETT   That's them out of harm's way. And now to the stockade. All aboard for Treasure Island.

(The SQUIRE, JIM LARD, LIVESEY and SMOLLETT leave. MRS H and RUBY come to front of stage and curtains close.)

MRS H   We'll enjoy the responsibility. Us girls just wanna have fun!

Song 13 –   **Girls Just Wanna Have Fun**

I come home in the morning light

My mother says when you gonna live your life right

Oh mother dear we're not the fortunate ones

And girls they want to have fun

Oh girls just want to have fun

The phone rings in the middle of the night

My father yells what you gonna do with your life

Oh daddy dear you know you're still number one

But girls they want to have fun

Oh girls just want to have –

That's all they really want

Some fun

When the working day is done

Girls – they want to have fun

Oh girls just want to have fun

Some boys take a beautiful girl

And hide her away from the rest of the world

I want to be the one to walk in the sun

Oh girls they want to have fun

Oh girls just want to have

That's all they really want

Some fun

When the working day is done

Girls – they want to have fun

Oh girls just want to have fun,

They want to have fun,

They want to have fun....

RUBY   Look Mrs H., they're secure in the hold. What say we too go to the island?

MRS H   Good idea Ruby. Let's follow and see what's occurring!

END OF SCENE

TREASURE ISLAND

ACT II

SCENE 2

The Stockade, which consists of a wooden wall to the rear of the stage with a clearing in front. The DOCTOR, JIM LARD, SMOLLETT and the SQUIRE enter with guns and bags of provisions.

LIVESEY	This was a good idea.
SMOLLETT	With its fortifications, our supplies and a spring of fresh water, we will be able to defend ourselves.
	(Enter MRS H and RUBY, with JW)
	Madam! You are supposed to be guarding the ship!
MRS H	Oh it's all locked up tight. Don't worry about it. We didn't want to miss out on all the action, that's all.
RUBY	Look who we found on the island. Wandering about on her own.
MRS H	This looks a dangerous place for a girl to be out all by herself.
JW	It goes against the principles of my job that there should be areas with restricted access.
SMOLLETT	We can't have you wandering around willy-nilly. You had better remain here in the stockade with us.
JW	Before we go any further, I suggest an immediate risk assessment be made. This looks a precarious place. We seem to be very exposed, and surrounded by dangers.
SMOLLETT	Can I remind you that technically you are under my command, and it is my responsibility to safeguard the

welfare of everyone here. We will be safe if we are careful.

SQUIRE   Above all, we need to be vigilant. If you ladies insist on remaining here then you must play your part. Ruby, you take the first watch with young Jim Lard.

RUBY   Yes, Sir. Come on young Jim, over here. I've still got the pistol. We'll take care of any intruders.

JW   All I ask is that you be careful. Consider the risks. Anticipate the problems, and have a carefully considered action plan for all eventualities.

RUBY   Oh I've got a plan alright! If anyone makes a move out there, they'll get a gut full of lead from me.

JW   Yes, well, that wasn't quite what I had in mind.

SQUIRE   Mrs H., you see to some food, but small portions only. We do not know how long it has to last.

MRS H   Yes, sir. I'll be really frugal.

JW   And what shall I do?

SQUIRE   I'm sure you have some paper work to catch up on. Create an evidence trail, that sort of thing.

JW   Will nobody take my work seriously?

(Shots and screams offstage.)

JIM LARD   What was that?

JW   That sounded like gun shots!

SMOLLETT   Silver's crew must have had a disagreement.

JW   And someone was shot?!

LIVESEY   These are desperate people. Gold fever has a curious influence on personality. They will stop at nothing. We must be on our guard.

SMOLLETT	It will be dark shortly. We must be very watchful tonight.
RUBY	Sir! Captain! I can see a white flag.
LIVESEY	Well, who is it?
SQUIRE	It looks like Silver, and three of his cronies.
JIM LARD	It's Cutthroat Katy, Handbag Jones and Pearl Plank.
SMOLLETT	*(Calling out)*That's far enough. State your business from there.

(The pirates appear on the side of the stage. PEARL is holding a white handkerchief tied to a stick.)

KATY	Captain Silver has a proposition for you.
SMOLLETT	*Captain* Silver is it now! You're the ship's mate, a self promoted sea cook.
SILVER	The men voted me captain after you all ....er .... deserted.
SMOLLETT	Deserted! You rogues and villains. I'll see you hang for this!
SILVER	Enough of this. Will you listen or not?
LIVESEY	We pay no attention to pirates!
SMOLLETT	No, let him speak. Go ahead Mr. Silver.
SILVER	Cap'n Silver, if you don't mind. We offer to guarantee your safety in exchange for the map. We will leave you plenty of food, and notify the first ship we see of your presence on Treasure Island.
LIVESEY	That's preposterous!
KATY	Yes. I agree. We thought it was very generous too.
PEARL	It would be much easier to kill you all.

HANDBAG	And much more fun too!
KATY	And who would know?
SILVER	You can see my comrades are restless. They know what's in the offing.
SMOLLETT	Well, Silver. I listened to you. Now you pay attention to me.
SILVER	You agree that we have been very fair?
SMOLLETT	I accept no such thing! I offer you a fair trial – the charge will be mutiny, and if you continue to resist, I'll see that you hang when we return to Falmouth.
SILVER	*(angry)* You leave me no option. My kindness has been ignored. We will take the stockade by force, at great cost to human lives – your lives. I bid you good day, gentlemen.
	(The pirates leave)
LIVESEY	*(to SMOLLETT)* You have my admiration, sir. To stand up to Silver took courage. More courage will be needed if they attack.
RUBY	Look out! Take cover! Get down!
	(Everyone ducks down, except JW, who looks bewildered. Shots are fired from offstage,and JW screams and falls down, clutching her arm.)
MRS H	After all her 'ealth 'n' safety concerns, she goes and get's herself shot!
	(JW groans in obvious pain)
RUBY	I know it must hurt.
JW	Not as much as knowing I won't get any compensation.
SQUIRE	Take care! We are still in grave danger!

(MRS H and RUBY drag JW behind the stockade and the others follow.)

SMOLLETT Only return fire if you are fired upon! *(More shots are fired and SMOLLETT collapses, shot in the arm.)*

SQUIRE Quick, Doctor Livesey, the Captain has been hit!

LIVESEY Your arm is shattered. I'll dress it and put it in a sling.

(While everyone is busy, JIM LARD slips out in front of the stockade. He is carrying a pistol.)

JIM LARD *(to himself)* I'm going to try and slip around the back of the pirates and see if I can pick one or two of them off.

(He creeps forward, the curtains close or a backdrop comes down, leaving him alone in front. A strange sea-shanty type song is being sung offstage.)

JIM LARD Silver's men sound to be drunk, judging by their singing.

(BEN GUNN appears briefly at the side of the stage.)

What was that? *(to audience)* Did you see anyone? You will tell me if you do, won't you?

(BEN GUNN appears again, then disappears.)

What was that? Behind me? There was someone behind me? *(turns full circle, first one way, then the other with BEN GUNN shadowing him)* There's no one there!

(BEN GUNN appears yet again and this time JIM LARD sees him.)

JIM LARD Don't move or I'll fire!

BEN GUNN *(putting his hands up)* Hold on lad, I mean you no 'arm.

JIM LARD Who are you? You weren't on the ship. Who are you?

BEN GUNN	My name is Ben Gunn.
JIM LARD	Well, I'm Jim Hawkins, known to one and all as Jim Lard. But what happened to you?
BEN GUNN	I was with Flint, when he buried the treasure. They painted me dark red and left me on the island.
JIM LARD	You don't mean ....
BEN GUNN	Yes I was marooned.
JIM LARD	Then you will know the sea cook with the artificial leg?
BEN GUNN	Silver?
JIM LARD	No. I think it was made of wood.
BEN GUNN	I know him all right. He sailed with Flint. He's an evil, vicious man. You'd better watch out for him.
JIM LARD	If we can escape from the pirates, we can take you back with us.
BEN GUNN	I've been ten years on this island, all alone. You haven't got a piece of cheese have you? I haven't tasted cheese for seven years! Oh, I'd love a piece of cheese!
JIM LARD	Cheese? Is that all you want after all this time?
Song 14–	**Cheese**
BEN GUNN	(solo, *sung to the tune of Charles Azanavour's "She"*)

Cheese may be the thing I can't forget

A trace of pleasure or regret

May be the treasure

Or the price I have to pay

Cheese may be the song that summer sings

May be the chill that autumn brings

May be a hundred different things

Within the measure of a day

Cheese may be the beauty or the beast

May be the famine or the feast

May turn each day into a heaven or a hell

Gorgonzola, Danish Blue,

Wensleydale and Edam too

Double Gloucester, Cheddar, Yarg

Stilton, Brie and Emmental.

Cheese may be the reason I survive

The why and wherefore I'm alive

The one I'll care for

Through the rough and ready years

Cheese, I'll take the laughter and the tears

And make them all my souvenirs

For where Cheese goes I've got to be

The meaning of my life is Cheese

Cheese may be the love that cannot hope to last

May come to me from shadows of the past

That I'll remember till the day I die

Gorgonzola, Danish Blue,

Wensleydale and Edam too

Double Gloucester, Cheddar, Yarg

Stilton, Brie and Emmental.

JIM LARD	I think there's some in the stockade. I'll go back and fetch some for you.
BEN GUNN	Before you go, you could help me finish my crossword. I've been searching for a word for ten years.
JIM LARD	Ten years – have you tried 'decade'?
BEN GUNN	Now try this one. Six letters, 'intense dislike'.
JIM LARD	That's horror. H O R, R O R.
BEN GUNN	Spell it like a pirate, Jim Lard.
JIM LARD	Oh, all right. Aitch, oh arrgh, arrgh oh arrgh!
BEN GUNN	That's it! Brilliant! Now, I'll wait near Spyglass Hill. You go and fetch your mates. But be careful, there's danger everywhere.

(BEN GUNN exits. JIM LARD sneaks back through the curtains, or the backdrop rises and he is back at the stockade. The pirates are lurking to one side of the stage)

SILVER	Who's that?

(SILVER traps JIM LARD with his crutch)

Well, Jim Lard. It's nice to see you. To see you.....

PIRATES	Nice!
JIM LARD	But where are my friends? What have you done with them?
KATY	Wouldn't you like to know!

JIM LARD:	You've killed them! I'll get you for this!
	(JIM tries to attack KATY, but is held at arms' reach)
KATY	Now don't be a silly little boy!
PEARL	Now we have you, we can make a start right now and go to look for the treasure.
JIM LARD	But you don't know where to look!
SILVER	This piece of paper should help! *(He takes the map from his pocket)* Five paces west.
JIM LARD	The map! How did you get hold of it?
SILVER	Your friends left it behind in their rush to leave. So now we're going to look for the treasure. *(He looks at the map)* I'll read the instructions. Handbag! Mark out the paces on the ground. *(reading the instructions on the map.)* Five paces west.
HANDBAG	One …two…three…er… four…What's next?
KATY	Five, you fool!
SILVER	And now five paces north.
KATY	You walk, Handbag, and I'll count. One, two, three, four, five.
SILVER	Now five east.
KATY	One, two, three, four, five.
SILVER	And finally, five paces south.
KATY	One, two, three, four, five.But she's back where she started!
SILVER	Flint always did have a strange sense of humour.
KATY	He didn't write this script did he?

SILVER	Jim Lard, you can help us dig.
JIM LARD	But there's a hole already here. The treasure's gone. Someone has beaten you to it!
KATY	Silver? What's this all about? You double crossing, one legged no good son of the sea!
	(both KATY and PEARL raise their guns)
SILVER	Now let's not be too 'asty. Don't do anything silly ladies. *(He holds JIM LARD in front of him, like a shield)*
PEARL	He must have sneaked out in the night. He's taken the gold and hidden it. He'll kill us all and keep the gold to himself! He's double crossed us!
HANDBAG	Right Silver, prepare to die. And you too, young Jim Lard!
	(Three shots are fired from offstage, KATY, HANDBAG and PEARL fall dead)
	(Enter DOCTOR, SQUIRE, SMOLLETT, MRS H, RUBY, BEN GUNN and JW. Both SMOLLETT and JW have an arm in a sling.)
JIM LARD	Oh, thank you for saving us! But where is the treasure?
SQUIRE	*(pointing to BEN GUNN.)* This man moved the treasure to his cave years ago. He thought it a safer place. He came and told us his story after he had met you.
JIM LARD	But no one told me!
LIVESEY	We didn't know if we could trust you. When you left yesterday, we all thought you had joined the pirates.
JIM LARD	I wouldn't do anything like that!
SQUIRE	Gold can do strange things to people.
SILVER	*(pretending to be humble)* I ought to thank you gentlemen,

for saving my life too. I was really on your side all the time. Just tried to trick them, that's all!

MRS H   A likely story.

SILVER   But what happens now?

SMOLLETT   Back to Falmouth, with Ben Gunn and the treasure, and I promise you a fair trial when we return.

SILVER   And that is the limit to your kindness?

LIVESEY   In the circumstances, we have been very generous. We could just shoot you for piracy, you know.

SILVER   So my pirate days are over.

JIM LARD   *(Running to the side of the stage)* Sir! There appears to be a ship's sail!

SMOLLETT   Then run along and see if you can get anything cheap!

LIVESEY   It's good to see you're feeling better, Smollett.

               (Curtains close behind them and they range along the front of the stage)

Song 15 –   **Gold Is The Colour**

               (sung to the tune of 'Blue is the Colour, Chelsea F.C. song from the 1970s)

               Gold is the colour, treasure is the name.

               We're out to find it, to find it is our aim.

               So cheer us on through the sun and rain,

               For treasure, treasure is the name.

               Down in the boats to the sandy shore

               We will search for hours and more.

'Til we have found what was buried there

Flint's treasure everywhere.

(chorus)

Come on the ship, and we'll welcome you

Wear your patch and see us through

Sing loud and clear 'til the treasure's won

Sing 'treasure' everyone.

(chorus repeat)

END OF SCENE.

TREASURE ISLAND

ACT II

SCENE 3

Back at the Admiral Benbow Inn. All those who were singing in the last song, are now sitting in the tavern, drinking. SILVER is disguised and sitting in a wheelchair in the corner of the stage, with a blanket over his legs. JW is also sitting with him, wearing dark glasses and a big hat. MRS H and RUBY are behind the bar. JIM LARD is standing centre stage, with a tray.

JIM LARD	*(To audience)* Well, we're back home. What an adventure! We found the treasure and brought it back with us. We rescued Ben Gunn and returned him to civilisation.
MRS H	I'm not sure that civilisation was ready for him, though.
	(BEN GUNN comes rushing out of the upstage right door, clutching a large wedge of cheese. He cackles, looks at the audience and says "Cheese!" loudly, then rushes out of the upstage left door.)
RUBY	It took him some time to adjust.
SQUIRE	You're all probably wandering what happened to everyone else.
	(Enter CAPTAIN SMOLLETT)
SMOLLETT	I can tell you about Silver as I have just returned from the court. We clapped him in irons as soon as we reached shore and he was charged with mutiny. He was in jail awaiting trial, but yesterday morning his cell was found empty. Goodness knows where he is now, or what he is doing. But

if he's any sense, he'll keep well clear of here. We'd all
recognise him, with one eye, one hand and one leg.

LIVESEY   He'll have great difficulty in disguising himself!

SMOLLETT   The strange thing is, the guards said he had a visitor late last
night. By the description, I'd say it was that Jobsworth
woman. What she wanted with him I can't imagine. But
since then, no one has seen Silver. Nor Jobsworth, come to
think of it.

JIM LARD   He wasn't all bad, Captain. I kind of liked him, really.

RUBY   He was a villain, Jim Lard. Make no mistake about that!

JIM LARD   You'll want to know what happened to the treasure, and
whether it made us all rich. Unfortunately, there is a
confidentiality agreement, so all I can say is that despite all
the dangers, it was definitely worth it!

                *(JIM is interrupted by a shout from the corner of the bar. It
                is SILVER in a wheelchair, heavily disguised beneath a thick
                blanket)*

SILVER   *(surprisingly polite and respectful)* If it's not too much
trouble, young sir, may I have another drink, and one also
for my lady friend please?

LIVESEY   Who's that Jim Lard?

JIM LARD   Oh, they're new around here. They arrived yesterday
afternoon. They're just staying for a few days.

MRS H   Such a nice couple too. Not a minute's bother. He limps very
badly, but she is ever so kind, and helps him get about. She
pushes him everywhere, when they go out for walks. From
what little he said, he's some kind of war hero. He was
badly injured fighting for King and Country.

RUBY	Funny thing is, he's only got one hand, and he looks to have an artificial eye too. If I didn't know any better, I'd say it was Silver.
SMOLLETT	And I suppose she's Ms Jobsworth! Don't be ridiculous! What an imagination you've got Ruby! Silver will keep well away from us!
JIM LARD	*(Bringing two drinks to SILVER.)* Here are your drinks, sir. One for you and one for your lady friend.
SILVER	*(grabbing JIM's wrist and whispering hoarsely)* Can you keep a secret Jim Lard? I know where to find treasure! Pirates' gold! I've got a map Jim Lard which tells us where to look!
JW	It will be dangerous and full of hazards – but that's what makes life so exciting, don't you think?
JIM LARD	Oh, no! Not again! Leave me alone! Leave me alone! I never want to see another treasure map as long as I live!

REPEAT OF GOLD IS THE COLOUR (2 CHORUSES) WITH KEY CHANGE

Song 16– I Just Can't Get You Out Of My Head

(Everyone starts singing and doing the robot moves that go with this Kylie song. Gradually, the rest of the cast come on stage and join in.)

GO ON STAGE WITH 3 DEAD PIRATES

EVERYONE	La la la
	La la la la la
	La la la
	La la la la la
	I just can't get you out of my head
	Boy your treasure is all I think about

I just can't get you out of my head

Boy it's more than I dare to think about

La la la

La la la la la

I just can't get you out of my head

Boy your treasure is all I think about

I just can't get you out of my head

Boy it's more than I dare to think about

JW   *(to SILVER)* Every night

Every day

Just to be there in your arms

Won't you stay

Won't you lay

Stay forever and ever and ever and ever

EVERYONE   La la la

La la la la la

La la la

La la la la la

I just can't get you out of my head

Boy your treasure is all I think about

I just can't get you out of my head

Boy it's more than I dare to think about

SILVER   *(to JW)* There's a dark secret in me

                Don't leave me locked in your heart

                Set me free

                Feel the need in me

                Set me free

                Stay forever and ever and ever and ever

EVERYONE   La la la

                La la la la la

                La la la

                La la la la la

                I just can't get you out of my head

                I just can't get you out of my head

                I just can't get you out of my head

                (Everyone freezes in strange positions on the final word of the song. BLACKOUT.)

                (Suggestions for curtain call are that everyone disappears and Mike Oldfield's Portsmouth is played as the individual players come back on. Rhythmic audience clapping should be encouraged.)

THE END.

FURNITURE LIST

Act 1

throughout: A wooden 'bar' surface for serving drinks; two or three small wooden tables (or barrels serving as tables); wooden stools or chairs (no more than six as most of the pirates should stand.)

Act II Scene 1:   A ' ship's wheel'; various large barrels dotted about; some 'rigging' (SEE SET PLAN 2)

Act II Scene 2:   Some foliage to suggest the island. (SEE SET PLAN 3)

PROPERTY LIST

ACT I start: On the bar - Large jugs of ale; many tankards; small 'tot' glasses; a ship's bell on the bar; bottles of 'rum'.

Under the bar – a drum and stick; a pot of single cream; a pair of spectacles.

Personal props – HANDBAG has a handbag; JIM LARD, RUBY and MRS H have tea towels and dishcloths.

Page 6:   JW enters with a hard hat and a clipboard.

Page 10:   JW enters with a whistle.

Page 13:   LIVESEY enters with a medical bag containing a stethoscope and a clipboard.

Page 19:   BONES enters with a knife in his pocket.

Page 24:   LIVESEY exits with his medical bag, clipboard and stethoscope.

JW enters and hands out leaflets.

Page 26:   PEARL enters with a leather pouch full of 'dust.'

ACT I
SCENE 1

Start: As before but cream, drum and stick have been removed. Golf club is under the bar.

BONES should have a key around his neck and coins in his pocket.

Page 35:   BLIND PEW enters with a white stick and the folded up 'black spot'.

Page 37:   JIM LARD appears with map.

SQUIRE and LIVESEY appear with pistols.

ACT 1
SCENE 3:   As before but golf club, map and black spot have been removed.

Large sign on display (SEE SCRIPT).

Page 48:   HANDBAG produces a dagger.

Page 49:   JW appears with lots of forms.

SILVER produces a filthy handkerchief.

ACT II

SCENE 1:	Pirates are loading supplies (sacks, small barrels etc.)
Start:	MRS H has a basket of cleaning supplies and a pair of pink long johns.
	RUBY has a clipboard.
	JW is hidden in the apple barrel with a clipboard, pen,
	Sight chart and wet floor sign (SEE SCRIPT).
	A washing line (with some clothes on) needs to be tied up at the side of the stage ready to be strung out on page 57.
	A telescope needs to be placed on stage for both SILVER and SMOLLETT to use.
Page 58:	MRS H, RUBY, JW and female pirates produce (from offstage) buckets, mops, washing basket with clothes and pegs.
Page 63:	Song 12 – audience participation. *You may wish to hand out song sheets here, or at the start of the play. Or you may wish to hand out other items to the audience, like sweets or flags to wave etc.*
Page 64:	SQUIRE draws a pistol.
Page 65:	LIVESEY or SMOLLETT gives RUBY a pistol.

ACT II

Scene 2

Page 67:	DOCTOR and others enter with guns and sacks of provisions.
Page 69:	Pirates enter carrying pistols. PEARL has a white handkerchief tied to a stick.

Page 71:   `JIM LARD has a pistol.

Page 75:   SILVER has the map in his pocket.

Page 76:   KATY, PEARL and HANDBAG have pistols.

                    SMOLLETT and JW are wearing arm slings.

ACT II

SCENE 3   All the Admiral Benbow Inn props for ACT I.

                    SILVER is in a wheel/bath chair.

Page 79:   BEN GUNN enters clutching a large chunk of cheese (or
                    two).

LIGHTING and EFFECTS

ACT I

SCENE 1

Page 1:   LIGHTS: *up.*

                    SFX: *Music. Admiral Benbow Inn. I verse and 1 chorus,*
                    then Pause.

                    CUE: MRS H: "This is verse two!"

                    SFX: *Music. Admiral Benbow Inn to end.*

Page 8:   CUE: BONES: My days at sea are over, more's the pity."

                    SFX: *Music. A-Rovin. To end.*

Page 13:   CUE: LIVESEY: "Well here's to the marvels of modern

                    medicine. Cheers!"

                    SFX: *Music. Lily the Pink until end of page 14. Pause.*

Page 16:   CUE: LIVESEY: "Are you taking anything?"

SFX : *Music. Resume Lily the Pink until top of page 17. Pause.*

Page 18:   CUE: LIVESEY: "No. Ten, nine, eight, seven…"

    SFX: *Music. Resume Lily the Pink until middle of page 19.*

Page 21:   CUE: MRS H: "But what shall we do with him?"

    SFX: *Music. What Shall We Do With A Drunken Sailor? Until bottom of page 23.*

Page 27:   CUE: BLACK DOG: "We'll just have to keep a watch on him over the next few days."

    SFX: *Music. We'll be Watching You until end of scene.*

Page 30:   CUE: end of song.

    LIGHTS: *Blackout.*

ACT I SCENE 2

Page 31:   LIGHTS: *Fade up.*

    SFX: *Music. Wild Rover until…*

    CUE : line of song "such a custom as you I can have any day."

    SFX: *Pause Wild Rover.*

Page 32:   CUE: ALL: "Shut up you silly woman!"

    SFX: *Resume Wild Rover until top of page 33.*

Page 37:   CUE: BLACK DOG (offstage): "Let's get him!"

    SFX: *Pistol shot offstage.*

    CUE: BLACK DOG (offstage): "Curse you – you interfering landlubber!"

SFX: *Two pistol shots offstage.*

Page 39:   CUE: RUBY: "Money, money and more money!"

SFX: *Music. Money, Money, Money until…*

Page 41:   CUE : Line of song – "my life will never be the same"

SFX: *Pause music.*

Page 42:   CUE: LIVESEY: "To Falmouth then, to hire a ship!"

SFX: *Resume song until end.*

CUE: End of song.

LIGHTS: *Blackout.*

ACT I SCENE 3

Page 43:   LIGHTS: *up.*

SFX: *Music. Blow The Man Down until end on page 44.*

Page 47:   CUE: SILVER: "The female of the species is deadlier than the male."

SFX: *Music. The Female of The Species is Deadlier than the Male until end on page 48.*

Page 52:   CUE: SMOLLETT: "We sail on tomorrow's tide."

SFX: *Music. Sailing until end on same page.*

LIGHTS: *Fade during last two lines of the song, then Blackout. Interval music if used. HOUSE LIGHTS UP.*

ACT II SCENE 1

Page 53: Suggested SFX before lights go up: *Waves and seagulls.*

LIGHTS : *up.*

SFX: *Music. Reprise of Sailing until end on page 54.*

Page 58: CUE: MRS H: "We'll get this sorted, and leave below decks for another day."

SFX: *Music. Sisters Are Doing It For Themselves until end on page 60.*

Page 62: CUE: SMOLLETT: "Lower the boat!"

SFX: *Music. Row, Row, Row the Boat. (may wish to pause music at certain points to allow actors to engage with audience.)*

LIGHTS: *May wish to bring House Lights up for audience participation.*

Page 65: CUE: MRS H: "Us girls just wanna have fun."

SFX: *Music. Girls Just Wanna Have Fun until end on page 66.*

Page 66: CUE: MRS H: "Let's follow and see what's occurring."

LIGHTS: *Blackout.*

ACT II SCENE 2

Page 67: Suggested SFX before lights go up: *Jungle sounds or exotic birds.*

LIGHTS: *Fade up.*

Page 68: CUE: JW: "Will nobody take my work seriously?"

SFX: *Two gun shots offstage.*

Page 70:   CUE: RUBY: "Take cover! Get down!"

SFX: *Several shots fired offstage.*

Page 71:   CUE: SMOLLETT: "Only return fire if you are fired upon!"

SFX: *Several shots fired on and off stage.*

CUE: JIM LARD: "...see if I can pick one or two of them off."

SFX: *Sea shanty is sung offstage.*

Page 72:   CUE: JIM LARD: "Cheese? Is that all you want after all this time?"

SFX: Music. *Cheese (She) which continues until end on page 74.*

Page 76:   CUE: HANDBAG: "And you too, Jim Lard."

SFX: *Three shots are fired offstage.*

Page 77:   CUE: LIVESEY: "It's good to see you're feeling better, Smollett."

SFX: *Music. Gold (Blue) is The Colour until end on page 78.*

Page 78:   CUE: end of song.

LIGHTS: *Blackout.*

ACT II SCENE 3

Page 79:   LIGHTS: *up.*

Page 81:   CUE: JIM LARD: "I never want to see another treasure map as long as I live."

SFX: *Music. I Just Can't Get You Out of My Head which continues until the end on page 83.*

Page 83:   CUE: end of song.

LIGHTS: *Blackout.*

SFX : *Curtain call music. (SEE SCRIPT).*

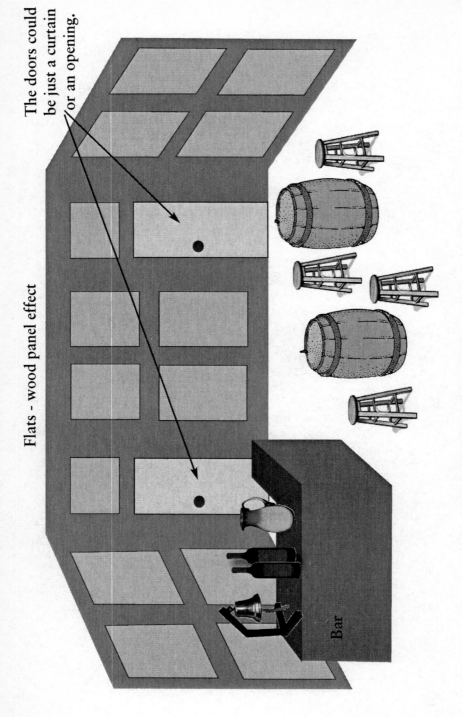

Flats - wood panel effect

The doors could be just a curtain or an opening.

Bar

SUGGESTED SET PLAN 1 – The Admiral Benbow Inn

SUGGESTED SET PLAN 2 – The ship

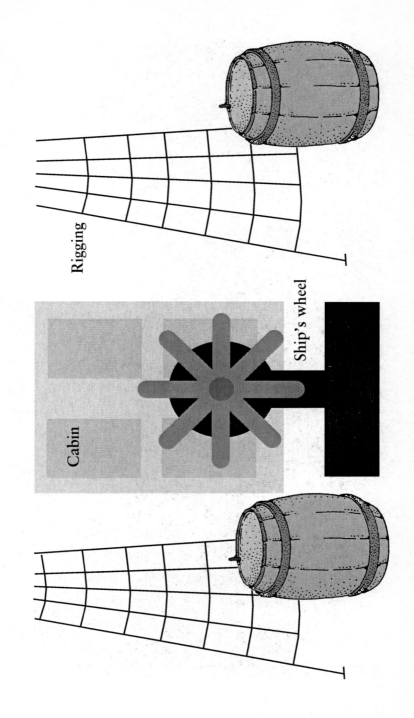

Rigging

Cabin

Ship's wheel

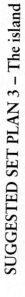

Timber stockade

Front flats with tropical foliage

SUGGESTED SET PLAN 3 – The island

Is your drama group tired of not being able to cast plays?

Do you suffer from a lack of young actors?

HELP HAS FINALLY ARRIVED!

Playstage Senior is a new publishing house totally devoted to creating new plays for experienced amateur actors. Our plays have some of the best parts for actors aged 40 to 70+ that you are ever going to find.

We guarantee that:

- You will never again have to waste your best actors in bit parts or supporting roles.
- You will never again have to scrabble around borrowing young actors from another group.
- Your older actors will never again be relegated to playing elderly relatives/butlers/housekeepers.
- We even have plays that have lead roles for 70 year olds – and not a Zimmer frame in sight!

We don't believe that the best new dramatic writing should only be for young actors.

Visit our website and have a good look at our catalogue. We have One Act and Full Length plays – dramas, comedies, farces and classic adaptations. Our inaugural list is small but choice and it is expanding all the time. All our play sets should be available to read in your local drama libraries. Let us know if they are not and we will rectify the situation. You can buy plays through our website or order them from your local bookshop. Application forms for performance licences are also available.

We're breaking new ground here. Grab a shovel and dig in!

www.playsforadults.com

If you would prefer a catalogue by post please send a stamped addressed A5 envelope to
Playstage, P.O. Box 52, AXMINSTER, EX13 5WB.

P.O.Box 52 AXMINSTER EX13 5WB
Tel: (UK) 01297 32905
EMAIL: mail@schoolplaysandpantos.com

PLAYS FOR SCHOOLS AND YOUTH GROUPS

www.schoolplaysandpantos.com

NO PERFORMANCE FEES

Playstage Junior was started in 2002 by Lynn Brittney, a former drama teacher and playwright. Since then, Playstage Junior plays have been performed in English-speaking classrooms all over the world – Australia; New Zealand; South Africa; Hong Kong; Eire; USA; Canada – as well as the UK. Purchasing and performing the plays couldn't be simpler. The website above allows you to look at samples of each play, purchase online in any currency and get an almost instant download of your chosen play. Or you can print out an order form and send a cheque in the mail. Production notes are included, to help teachers and leaders make scenery, costumes and props. Once you purchase a play, you receive a licence to photocopy and the play is yours to reproduce and perform forever. Sheet music is also included, where applicable.

ONLY FOR USE BY BONA FIDE SCHOOLS,
YOUTH GROUPS AND ORGANISATIONS.
THERE ARE NO PERFORMANCE FEES.